SOUTHERN BARBECUE & GRILLING

DANIEL SCHUMACHER

83 PRESS

SOUTHERN
BARBECUE
& GRILLING

GRUMPY'S
PRIVATE LABEL
Black Label
"Spicy" BBQ Sauce

83
PRESS

Copyright © 2017 by 83 Press

83 Press
1900 International Park Drive, Suite 50
Birmingham, Alabama 35243
www.hoffmanmedia.com

ISBN #978-1-940772-38-7
Printed in China

contents

INTRODUCTION

Barbecue may not have been invented in the American South, but Southerners have worked hard to perfect it. In a relentless pursuit of the tenderest pork, chicken, and beef, generations of hardworking Southerners have tended coals, adjusted smokers, and stewarded the meat to its perfect state. These humble folks started with the simplest ingredients on earth—meat and fire—and added rubs, sauces, and smoke to the mix as time went on, elevating it to an art.

Whether charcoal, gas, or wood burning, our backyard grills and barbecue pits offer endless options for culinary delight beyond traditional barbecue. Kebabs, steaks, hamburgers, seafood, and more benefit from high-heat direct cooking, and low-and-slow marathon sessions.

Fire up your grill, gather the family, and get ready for some of the best barbecue you have ever had.

CHAPTER ONE

Barbecue

BARBECUE, SAUCES AND SPICES

SMOKED BEEF BRISKET

For an authentic smoke ring, be sure to keep the environment in your
smoker moist by spritzing water on your brisket or basting it.

YIELD: 10 TO 12 SERVINGS

Mesquite wood chips, soaked in
   water for 30 minutes
⅓ cup kosher salt
2 tablespoons coarsely ground
   black pepper
2 tablespoons garlic salt
1 tablespoon ground chipotle
   chile pepper
1 (6-pound) flat-cut beef brisket,
   fat trimmed to ⅛ inch

Preheat smoker to 225° to 250°. Sprinkle wood chips over coals.

In a small bowl, stir together salt, black pepper, garlic salt, and chile pepper. Spread mixture over brisket. Place brisket fat side up in a disposable roasting pan. Let stand at room temperature for 30 minutes.

Cook, covered, for 5 hours. Remove brisket from pan; discard pan. Wrap brisket in heavy-duty foil. Return brisket to smoker. Cook, covered, until tender, 4 to 6 hours more. Let stand for 30 minutes.

BABY BACK RIBS

These tender ribs are worth the wait with their complex chili flavor and a hint of
sweetness from brown sugar. They'll be a showstopper at your next cookout.

YIELD: 4 TO 6 SERVINGS

5	tablespoons chili powder
¼	cup firmly packed light brown sugar
3	tablespoons kosher salt
2	tablespoons onion powder
1	tablespoon dry mustard
1	tablespoon smoked paprika
1	tablespoon ground black pepper
1	teaspoon garlic salt
2	(2½-pound) racks baby back ribs

In a medium bowl, stir together chili powder, brown sugar, salt, onion
powder, mustard, paprika, pepper, and garlic salt.

Using a sharp knife, pierce thin membrane on back of ribs. Peel to remove;
discard. Rub chili powder mixture over ribs. Wrap ribs in plastic wrap;
refrigerate for at least 8 hours or up to 24 hours.

Let ribs come to room temperature. Remove plastic wrap, and wrap ribs in
heavy-duty foil.

Preheat one side of grill to low heat (250° to 300°).

Grill over indirect heat, covered, turning occasionally, until very tender,
6 to 8 hours.

ALABAMA SMOKED CHICKEN

The versatility and heartiness of this bird will
make it a "regular" at your cookouts.

⚓

YIELD: APPROXIMATELY 4 SERVINGS

BRINE
4   cups water
¼   cup sugar
¼   cup salt

ALABAMA WHITE SAUCE
1   cup mayonnaise
½   cup whole buttermilk
½   cup distilled white
      vinegar
1½ teaspoons ground
      black pepper

¼   teaspoon kosher salt
¼   teaspoon sugar

CHICKEN
1   (4½- to 5-pound)
      whole chicken
½   teaspoon kosher salt
¼   teaspoon ground black
      pepper
Apple wood chips, soaked
      in water for 30 minutes

FOR BRINE: In a medium saucepan, bring 4 cups water,
sugar, and salt to a boil over medium-high heat. Reduce
heat to medium-low; simmer until sugar and salt are
dissolved, approximately 3 minutes. Remove from heat,
and let cool completely.

FOR WHITE SAUCE: In a medium bowl, whisk together
all ingredients. Cover and refrigerate for up to 2 weeks.

FOR CHICKEN: Remove giblets from chicken, and
discard. Using kitchen scissors, cut along both sides of
backbone. Remove backbone, and discard. Cut through
center of breast to separate chicken into halves.

In a large airtight container, place chicken and brine.
Refrigerate for 8 hours. Remove chicken from brine;
discard brine. Pat chicken dry. Sprinkle both halves with
salt and pepper. Let stand for 30 minutes.

Preheat smoker to 225° to 250°. Sprinkle wood chips
over coals.

Cook chicken, skin side down, covered, for 1 hour.
Turn chicken over; cover and cook until a meat
thermometer inserted in thickest portion registers 165°,
approximately 1 hour and 45 minutes. Let stand for
10 minutes. Serve with Alabama White Sauce.

SMOKED PORK BUTT

This no-nonsense pork butt gets the low-and-slow treatment.

———————————— ⚓ ————————————

YIELD: 10 TO 12 SERVINGS

Cherry and maple wood chips
½ cup Basic Barbecue Rub
(recipe on page 26)
1 (10- to 11-pound) bone-in
Boston butt

Soak wood chips in water at least 30 minutes.

Preheat smoker to 225° to 250°. Sprinkle soaked wood chips over coals.

Spread Dry Rub evenly over all sides of pork. Let stand at room temperature 30 minutes.

Cook, with smoker lid closed, until a meat thermometer inserted in thickest portion reads 165°, approximately 5 hours. Remove pork from smoker, and wrap tightly in heavy-duty aluminum foil. Return pork to smoker, and cook, with smoker lid closed, until a meat thermometer inserted in thickest portion reads 190°, 4 to 5 hours more. Let stand 30 minutes. Shred pork, discarding fat.

MISSISSIPPI DELTA TAMALES

South of the border flavor meets the soul of the Mississippi Delta in these tamales. After the cooking is done, don't be shy with the fixin's—when hot sauce and barbecue sauce team up, good things happen.

＊

YIELD: APPROXIMATELY 18

FILLING

- 1¾ pounds smoked pulled pork, coarsely chopped
- 1 tablespoon chili powder
- 1½ teaspoons paprika
- 1½ teaspoons salt
- 1½ teaspoons garlic powder
- 1 teaspoon ground cumin
- 1 teaspoon ground red pepper

TAMALES

- 18 to 20 large dried cornhusks
- 5 cups instant masa
- 3¾ cups chicken broth, divided
- 1 cup lard or all-vegetable shortening
- 1 tablespoon baking powder
- 1¼ teaspoons salt
- Garnish: chopped green onion, chopped white onion, hot sauce, barbecue sauce

FOR FILLING: In a large bowl, stir together pork, chili powder, paprika, salt, garlic powder, cumin, and red pepper.

FOR TAMALES: In a large bowl, cover cornhusks with hot water, and let stand for 1 hour. Drain.

In the bowl of a stand mixer fitted with the paddle attachment, beat masa, 3 cups broth, lard, baking powder, and salt at medium speed until a soft dough forms.

Remove 1 husk from bowl, shaking off excess water. Place husk on a work surface. Place ⅓ cup dough in center of husk. Using dampened fingers, press dough into a 5x4-inch rectangle. Scatter ¼ cup pork filling down center of dough. Fold over one long side of husk, overlapping dough to encase pork mixture. Press long edges of husks together; fold over toward center. Fold narrow end of husk up toward center; tie with kitchen twine. Repeat procedure with remaining husks, dough, and filling. (If dough becomes dry, add remaining ¾ cup broth, 3 tablespoons at a time, to moisten.)

In a large stockpot, place a large metal collapsible steamer basket. Add water to fill just below bottom of basket. Arrange tamales, open end up, in basket. Bring to a boil; reduce heat to medium-low. Cover and simmer until masa dough feels firm, approximately 1 hour. (Use a measuring cup to add additional water to stockpot as needed.) Garnish with green onion, white onion, hot sauce, and barbecue sauce, if desired.

TEXAS-STYLE BEEF RIBS

Bring a little bit of the Lone Star State to the grill with these beef ribs.

—⚓—

YIELD: APPROXIMATELY 6 SERVINGS

MOPPING SAUCE

1	cup ketchup
½	cup apple cider vinegar
2	tablespoons Worcestershire sauce
1	teaspoon onion powder
1	teaspoon garlic powder
1	teaspoon ground cumin

BEEF RIBS

3	tablespoons kosher salt
2	tablespoons firmly packed dark brown sugar
1	tablespoon onion powder
1	tablespoon smoked paprika
1	teaspoon dry mustard
1	teaspoon dried thyme
1	teaspoon dried basil
1	teaspoon ground cumin
2	(2- to 3-pound) racks beef spare ribs

FOR MOPPING SAUCE: In a small bowl, combine all ingredients. Cover and refrigerate until grilling.

FOR BEEF RIBS: In a small bowl, combine salt, brown sugar, onion powder, paprika, mustard, thyme, basil, and cumin.

Using a sharp knife, pierce thin membrane on back of ribs. Peel to remove; discard. Rub salt mixture over ribs. Let stand at room temperature for 30 minutes. Spray grill rack with nonflammable cooking spray. Preheat one side of grill to low (250° to 300°).

Grill, meaty side down, over indirect heat, covered, for 2 hours, brushing every 30 minutes with Mopping Sauce. Turn ribs over, and cook, covered, until tender, 3 to 4 hours more, brushing every 30 minutes with Mopping Sauce.

SWEET & SMOKY BOSTON BUTT

This tender pork butt is delicious on its own and shines in sandwiches.

——————————— ⚓ ———————————

YIELD: 10 TO 12 SERVINGS

SWEET & SMOKY RUB

- ¼ cup kosher salt
- ¼ cup firmly packed light brown sugar
- ¼ cup smoked paprika
- 2 tablespoons granulated sugar
- 2 tablespoons ground black pepper
- 1 tablespoon onion powder
- 1 tablespoon garlic powder
- 1 tablespoon dry mustard
- 2 teaspoons celery salt
- 2 teaspoons ground cumin
- 2 teaspoons dried thyme

BOSTON BUTT

- Oak wood chips, soaked in water for 30 minutes
- 1 (7- to 8-pound) bone-in Boston butt

FOR RUB: In a small bowl, combine all ingredients. Store in an airtight container for up to 1 month.

FOR BOSTON BUTT: Preheat smoker to 225° to 250°. Sprinkle wood chips over coals.

Spread Sweet & Smoky Rub over all sides of pork. Let stand at room temperature for 30 minutes.

Cook, covered, until meat is very tender, 11 to 12 hours. Remove from smoker, and let stand for 30 minutes. Shred pork; discard fat.

SAUCES, SPICES, AND RUBS

BASIC BARBECUE RUB

YIELD: APPROXIMATELY 1½ CUPS

- ¼ cup smoked paprika
- ¼ cup firmly packed light brown sugar
- 3 tablespoons kosher salt
- 2 tablespoons onion powder
- 2 tablespoons garlic powder
- 2 tablespoons dry mustard
- 2 tablespoons chili powder
- 2 tablespoons ground black pepper
- 2 teaspoons ground red pepper

In a small bowl, combine all ingredients.

RIB RUB

In a small bowl, combine Basic Barbecue Rub, ¼ cup dried parsley, 2 tablespoons dried oregano, and 2 tablespoons lemon zest.
YIELD: APPROXIMATELY 2 CUPS

BRISKET RUB

In a small bowl, combine Basic Barbecue Rub, 2 tablespoons ground cumin, 2 tablespoons dried oregano, and 2 tablespoons ground black pepper.
YIELD: APPROXIMATELY 2 CUPS

CHICKEN RUB

In a small bowl, stir together Basic Barbecue Rub, 2 tablespoons fennel seed, 2 tablespoons celery seed, and 2 tablespoons ground ginger.
YIELD: APPROXIMATELY 2 CUPS

MEMPHIS-STYLE DRY RUB

YIELD: APPROXIMATELY 1 CUP

- ½ cup paprika
- ¼ cup firmly packed light brown sugar
- 2 tablespoons salt
- 1 tablespoon garlic powder
- 1 tablespoon ground black pepper
- 1 teaspoon celery salt
- ½ teaspoon ground red pepper

In a small bowl, combine all ingredients. Store in an airtight container for up to 2 months.

CLASSIC CAJUN SEASONING

YIELD: APPROXIMATELY ⅔ CUP

2 tablespoons garlic powder	2 teaspoons ground thyme
2 tablespoons onion powder	1 teaspoon ground cumin
2 tablespoons salt	½ teaspoon dry mustard
4 teaspoons Hungarian paprika	½ teaspoon ground celery seed
2 teaspoons ground black pepper	½ teaspoon ground chipotle chile pepper
2 teaspoons ground oregano	

In a small bowl, combine all ingredients. Store in an airtight container for up to 6 months.

SWEET AND SMOKY CAJUN SEASONING

YIELD: APPROXIMATELY ¾ CUP

2 tablespoons garlic powder	2 teaspoons ground oregano
2 tablespoons onion powder	2 teaspoons ground thyme
2 tablespoons salt	1 teaspoon ground cumin
4 teaspoons smoked paprika	½ teaspoon dry mustard
2 teaspoons ground black pepper	½ teaspoon mace
2 teaspoons ground Aleppo pepper	½ teaspoon ground celery seed
2 teaspoons ground dried green bell pepper	½ teaspoon ground chipotle chile pepper
2 teaspoons ground dried red bell pepper	½ teaspoon ground cardamom

In a small bowl, combine all ingredients. Store in an airtight container for up to 6 months.

SPICY CAJUN SEASONING

YIELD: APPROXIMATELY 1 CUP

2 tablespoons garlic powder	2 teaspoons ground jalapeño
2 tablespoons onion powder	2 teaspoons ground red pepper
2 tablespoons salt	2 teaspoons ground chipotle chile pepper
4 teaspoons chili powder	2 teaspoons ground oregano
2 teaspoons Hungarian paprika	2 teaspoons ground thyme
2 teaspoons ground black pepper	1 teaspoon ground cumin
2 teaspoons ground dried green bell pepper	½ teaspoon dry mustard
2 teaspoons ground dried red bell pepper	½ teaspoon ground celery seed

In a small bowl, combine all ingredients. Store in an airtight container for up to 6 months.

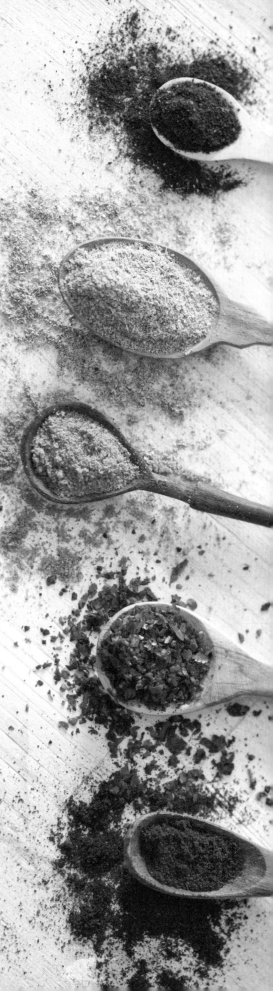

GREEN HOT SAUCE

YIELD: APPROXIMATELY 2 CUPS

1	fresh jalapeño, seeded and diced	1	tomatillo, hull removed and diced
½	fresh poblano, seeded and diced	1	kiwi, peeled
½	fresh Serrano, seeded and diced	¼	cup fresh lime juice
½	fresh Anaheim, seeded and diced	¼	cup water
		2	tablespoons distilled white vinegar
		1	tablespoon honey
		½	teaspoon salt

In the work bowl of a food processor or blender, combine all ingredients; process until completely smooth, 5 to 7 minutes. To reach desired consistency, add more water and vinegar. Transfer to a clean glass jar, and chill until ready to serve. Hot sauce will keep for up to 1 month.

SPICY RED HOT SAUCE

YIELD: APPROXIMATELY 3 CUPS

4	cups water	3	habañero, seeded and diced
1	tablespoon plus ½ teaspoon salt, divided	1	red Fresno chile pepper, seeded and diced
½	cup chopped carrot	½	cup distilled white vinegar
¼	cup diced onion	1	tablespoon tomato paste
3	cloves garlic	1¼	teaspoons sugar

In a Dutch oven, bring 4 cups water and 1 tablespoon salt to a boil. Add carrot, onion, and garlic; cook until tender, 8 to 10 minutes. Remove from heat, and let cool completely. Reserve water.

In the work bowl of a food processor or blender, place ¾ cup reserved water, cooked vegetables, habañero, chile pepper, vinegar, tomato paste, sugar, and remaining ½ teaspoon salt. Process until completely smooth, 5 to 7 minutes. To reach desired consistency, add more reserved water and vinegar, if desired. Transfer to a clean glass jar, and chill until ready to serve. Hot sauce will keep for up to 1 month.

RED RÉMOULADE

YIELD: APPROXIMATELY 1½ CUPS

¾	cup mayonnaise	1	tablespoon Creole mustard
2	tablespoons tomato paste	1	tablespoon Worcestershire sauce
2	tablespoons chopped capers	2	teaspoons red wine vinegar
2	tablespoons chopped fresh green onion	1	teaspoon Creole seasoning
1	tablespoon chopped fresh parsley	1	clove garlic, minced
		½	teaspoon celery salt
		¼	teaspoon kosher salt

In a large bowl, combine all ingredients. Cover and chill for up to 5 days.

WHITE RÉMOULADE

YIELD: APPROXIMATELY 2 CUPS

¾	cup mayonnaise	1	tablespoon chopped fresh chives
¼	cup Dijon mustard	1	tablespoon minced shallot
¼	cup whole-grain mustard	1½	teaspoons hot sauce
3	tablespoons chopped cornichons	1	teaspoon lemon zest
2	tablespoons prepared horseradish	2	teaspoons fresh lemon juice
2	tablespoons chopped fresh parsley	1	clove garlic, minced
		¼	teaspoon kosher salt

In a medium bowl, combine all ingredients. Cover and chill for up to 5 days.

CAROLINA MUSTARD SAUCE

YIELD: APPROXIMATELY 2 CUPS

1½	cups yellow mustard	1	tablespoon smoked paprika
½	cup apple cider vinegar	2	teaspoons Worcestershire sauce
⅓	cup firmly packed light brown sugar	1	teaspoon ground black pepper

In a medium bowl, combine all ingredients. Cover and chill for up to 5 days.

COOKED RED SAUCE

YIELD: APPROXIMATELY 2½ CUPS

1½	cups ketchup	2	tablespoons Worcestershire sauce
½	cup unsulphured molasses	2	teaspoons chili powder
¼	cup water	2	teaspoons liquid smoke
2	tablespoons apple cider vinegar	1	teaspoon ground black pepper

In a medium saucepan, combine all ingredients. Cook over medium-low heat, stirring occasionally, until slightly thickened, 15 to 20 minutes. Serve warm, or cover and chill for up to 5 days.

CAROLINA MUSTARD

COOKED RED SAUCE

CAROLINA VINEGAR SAUCE

CAROLINA VINEGAR SAUCE

YIELD: APPROXIMATELY 2 CUPS

1	cup apple cider vinegar	1	teaspoon dry mustard
¾	cup ketchup	½	teaspoon onion powder
2	tablespoons Worcestershire sauce	½	teaspoon garlic powder
1	tablespoon firmly packed light brown sugar	½	teaspoon celery salt
2	teaspoons kosher salt	½	teaspoon ground black pepper
		⅛	teaspoon ground red pepper

In a medium bowl, combine all ingredients. Cover and chill for up to 5 days.

WOOD: FUEL & FLAVOR

When smoking, wood plays many roles. It acts as a fuel and lends flavor as well as color to the meat. Instead of thinking of each wood as its own unique "spice," it can be helpful to look at all of them as a spectrum, from mild-tasting to intense, with the milder woods being more appropriate for lighter meats (like poultry), and ones that won't be heavily sauced. More assertive varieties including hickory and oak can hold their own against sauces, but be careful with mesquite. Many Texan pitmasters swear by mesquite, but its powerful flavor can hijack just about any meat.

SMOKING TEMPERATURE TIPS

- The temperature of the grill needs to be maintained at around 250°. This is achieved by making small adjustments to the top and bottom vents of the grill. Open the vents to raise the temperature; close them to lower the temperature.
- If the temperature drops dramatically, add some additional lit coals to the grill.
- Make sure you start smoking on a clean grill. Old ash can block the air vents and make temperature control difficult.

GRILL TO SMOKER
A STEP-BY-STEP GUIDE

1. Pile about 40 pieces of unlit hardwood lump charcoal* on one side of the grill. Place about 20 pieces of charcoal in a charcoal chimney, and light the chimney. Heat the coals until they have ashed over (turned gray).

2. Meanwhile, place a foil pan on the opposite side of the grill from the unlit coals. (The pan will catch any drippings from the meat.) With the pan in place, add the lit coals on top of the unlit coals. Add a handful of wood chips or chunks to the lit coals. Place the grate on the grill, close the lid, and wait for smoke, about 5 minutes.

3. Fill a foil loaf pan with water, and place on grill over coals. Cover grill; open bottom vent a quarter to halfway. Leave top vent almost completely closed (see Temperature Tips) until temperature reaches 250°. Add meat to unlit side of grill; cook as directed. Avoid opening grill lid.

Charcoal briquettes may be substituted.

WOOD FLAVOR PROFILE
Mild: Alder, Apple, Cherry, Peach, Pear
Medium: Hickory, Maple, Oak, Pecan
Strong: Mesquite

BEST ALL-PURPOSE
Apple, Cherry, Oak

SUGGESTED PAIRINGS
Apple and Hickory
Cherry and Maple
Pecan and Oak

FUN AND FLAVORFUL
Oak Wine Barrel Chips with Grapevines
   (from Barrel & Vines)
White oak TABASCO Wood Chips
   (from McIlhenny Company)
Jack Daniel's Wood Smoking Chips
   (from Jack Daniel's)

AVOID
Softwoods (such as Pine, Fir, Cypress,
Spruce, Redwood); lumber scraps (which
can be treated with chemicals); and wet
or moldy wood

CHAPTER TWO

Grilling

MEATS AND VEGGIES

CEDAR PLANK SNAPPER WITH GRILLED VEGETABLES

This quick fish dinner is as colorful as it is flavorful. Jalapeño,
poblano, and sweet peppers pack a punch and jazz up your plate.

YIELD: 6 SERVINGS

1 (15x6-inch) cedar plank, soaked
6 (6-ounce) snapper fillets
⅓ cup plus 2 tablespoons extra-virgin olive oil, divided
2 teaspoons kosher salt, divided
2 teaspoons ground black pepper, divided
1 (8-ounce) bag miniature sweet peppers
1 fresh jalapeño
1 fresh poblano
1 yellow onion, sliced
¼ cup fresh lime juice
1 tablespoon chopped fresh cilantro
Garnish: fresh cilantro, lime wedges

Spray grill rack with nonflammable cooking spray. Preheat grill to medium-high heat (350° to 400°).

Brush snapper fillets with ⅓ cup oil, and sprinkle with 1 teaspoon salt and 1 teaspoon black pepper.

In a medium bowl, combine sweet peppers, jalapeño, poblano, onion, and 1 tablespoon oil, tossing to combine.

Grill peppers and onion until charred. Set aside until cool enough to handle. Halve, seed, and chop sweet peppers. Chop onion and remaining peppers.

In a medium bowl, combine grilled vegetables, lime juice, cilantro, remaining 1 tablespoon oil, remaining 1 teaspoon salt, and remaining 1 teaspoon pepper.

Place cedar plank on grill. Grill snapper on plank until opaque and cooked through, 3 to 5 minutes per side. Serve with charred vegetables. Garnish with cilantro and lime wedges, if desired.

LEMON-BASIL SHRIMP

Served either as a side or a main dish, these petite crustaceans pack big, citrusy flavor.

YIELD: APPROXIMATELY 4 SERVINGS

¼ cup lemon pepper seasoning
4 teaspoons dried basil
2 teaspoons dried chervil
2 teaspoons ground fennel seed
1 teaspoon garlic powder
1 teaspoon kosher salt
½ teaspoon ground black pepper
1 pound peeled and deveined large fresh shrimp

In a small bowl, combine lemon pepper seasoning, basil, chervil, fennel, garlic powder, salt, and pepper. Transfer to a sealed container, and store for up to 6 months.

Spray grill rack with nonflammable cooking spray. Preheat grill to medium-high heat (350° to 400°).

Sprinkle shrimp with 2 tablespoons lemon-basil rub. Grill until pink and firm, about 2 minutes per side. Serve immediately.

GRILLED AMBERJACK PO'BOYS WITH MAQUE CHOUX

Don't let shrimp and oysters have all the fun! Grilled amberjack makes a delicious and elevated po' boy.

YIELD: 6 SERVINGS

2 tablespoons unsalted butter
1 (4-ounce) package diced pancetta
2 cups fresh corn kernels (from about 4 ears corn)
½ cup chopped onion
½ cup chopped green bell pepper
¼ cup chopped celery
1 tablespoon chopped fresh thyme leaves
1½ teaspoons salt, divided
4 cloves garlic, minced
3 tomatoes, seeded and diced
½ teaspoon ground black pepper
¼ teaspoon ground red pepper
6 (7-ounce) amberjack fillets
Olive oil, for brushing
1 tablespoon Cajun seasoning*
White Rémoulade (recipe on page 29)
2 (16-ounce) baguettes, sliced into 3 pieces each and split
Garnish: sliced green onion

In a large skillet, heat butter over medium-high heat for 6 to 8 minutes. Reduce heat to medium; add pancetta, corn, onion, bell pepper, celery, thyme, and 1 teaspoon salt. Cook, stirring frequently, until vegetables are tender, 15 to 20 minutes. Add garlic and tomatoes, and cook for 8 to 10 minutes. Add black pepper, red pepper, and remaining ½ teaspoon salt.

Spray grill rack with nonflammable cooking spray. Preheat grill to medium-high heat (350° to 400°).

Brush fillets with oil, and sprinkle with Cajun seasoning. Grill fish, turning once, until cooked through, 5 to 6 minutes.

Spread desired amount of White Rémoulade on 1 baguette piece. Add 1 fillet, and top with about ⅓ cup corn mixture. Repeat with remaining baguette pieces, White Rémoulade, corn mixture, and fillets. Garnish with green onion, if desired.

We used Slap Ya Mama Cajun Seasoning.

MUSTARD-ANCHO
NEW YORK STRIP STEAKS

Ancho chile pepper gives the New York strip steaks added complexity and heat.

⚜

YIELD: 4 SERVINGS

2 tablespoons dry mustard
1 tablespoon ground ancho chile pepper
1 tablespoon smoked paprika
2 teaspoons garlic powder
2 teaspoons celery salt
2 teaspoons kosher salt
1 teaspoon onion powder
1 teaspoon dried thyme
1 teaspoon ground black pepper
4 (8- to 10-ounce) New York strip steaks

In a small bowl, combine mustard, chile pepper, paprika, garlic powder, celery salt, salt, onion powder, thyme, and pepper. Transfer to a sealed container, and store for up to 6 months.

Spray grill rack with nonflammable cooking spray. Preheat grill to medium-high heat (350° to 400°).

Sprinkle 2 tablespoons rub over meat. Grill until desired degree of doneness, about 3 minutes per side for medium-rare. Serve immediately.

BLACK PEPPER-BRINED SMOKED TURKEY BREAST

Smoked to perfection over nutty pecan wood, this bird goes earthy with its herb and black pepper brine.

⚜

YIELD: 6 TO 8 SERVINGS

1   gallon hot water
1   cup kosher salt
½   cup firmly packed light brown sugar
¼   cup Worcestershire sauce
3   tablespoons ground black pepper
3   tablespoons minced garlic
1   tablespoon chopped fresh rosemary
1   tablespoon chopped fresh thyme
½   gallon ice
1   (6-pound) turkey breast
Pecan wood chips, soaked in water for 30 minutes

In a large container, stir together 1 gallon hot water, salt, and brown sugar until dissolved. Add Worcestershire, pepper, garlic, rosemary, thyme, and ice, stirring until ice is melted. Add turkey; cover and refrigerate for at least 8 hours or up to 12 hours.

Preheat smoker to 225° to 250°. Sprinkle wood chips over coals. Remove turkey from brine; discard brine. Pat turkey dry, and let stand at room temperature for 30 minutes.

Cook, covered, until a meat thermometer inserted in thickest portion registers 165°, about 2½ hours. Let stand for 10 minutes before slicing.

GRILLED TUNA SALAD

Cilantro vinaigrette is a flavorful choice, paired with fresh tuna and peppery baby arugula.

YIELD: 6 SERVINGS

CILANTRO VINAIGRETTE

- ¼ cup fresh lemon juice
- ¼ cup olive oil
- 1 tablespoon chopped fresh cilantro
- 1 tablespoon chopped fresh parsley
- 1 teaspoon salt
- ½ teaspoon ground black pepper

TUNA SALAD

- 1½ pounds sushi-grade tuna (about 2 inches thick)
- 3 tablespoons vegetable oil
- 1½ teaspoons kosher salt
- 1 teaspoon ground black pepper
- 1½ cups fresh baby arugula
- 1 seedless cucumber, peeled and sliced
- ¼ cup thinly sliced radish
- 1 avocado, sliced

FOR VINAIGRETTE: In the container of a blender, combine lemon juice, oil, cilantro, parsley, salt, and pepper; blend for 20 to 30 seconds. Use immediately, or cover and refrigerate for up to 1 week.

FOR TUNA SALAD: Spray grill rack with nonflammable cooking spray. Preheat grill to medium-high heat (350° to 400°).

Cut tuna into 2-inch-wide rectangles. Brush with oil to coat. Sprinkle with salt and pepper, pressing gently to adhere. Grill tuna, turning once, until ⅛-inch border is opaque but still very rare inside. Transfer tuna to a cutting board, and cut across the grain into ¼-inch slices.

In a medium bowl, combine arugula, cucumber, radish, and avocado. Add 3 tablespoons vinaigrette; toss gently to combine. Divide salad among serving plates. Top salad with tuna. Serve with remaining vinaigrette, if desired.

KITCHEN TIP:
To blanch potatoes and onions, cook potatoes in boiling salted water for 8 minutes. Add onions; cook 2 minutes more. Drain.

VEGETABLE KABOBS WITH DILL MARINADE

The vegetable medley options are endless with this kabob and dill marinade pairing.

YIELD: APPROXIMATELY 6 SERVINGS

DILL MARINADE
- ¾ cup olive oil
- ¼ cup Champagne vinegar
- 3 tablespoons chopped fresh dill
- 1 tablespoon minced garlic
- ¾ teaspoon kosher salt
- ½ teaspoon ground black pepper
- ¼ teaspoon sugar

KABOBS
- 1½ pounds new potatoes, blanched (see Kitchen Tip)
- ½ (10-ounce) package purple pearl onions, blanched and peeled
- ½ (10-ounce) package white pearl onions, blanched and peeled
- 3 medium zucchini, sliced 1 inch thick
- 4 medium yellow squash, sliced 1 inch thick
- 3 ears corn, sliced 1½ inches thick
- 4 to 6 radishes, trimmed
- 4 to 6 wooden skewers, soaked in water for 30 minutes
- 1 teaspoon kosher salt
- ½ teaspoon ground black pepper
- Garnish: fresh thyme

FOR DILL MARINADE: In a small bowl, whisk together oil and vinegar until smooth. Whisk in dill, garlic, salt, pepper, and sugar. Cover and refrigerate for up to 3 days.

FOR KABOBS: In a large bowl, stir together potatoes, onions, zucchini, squash, corn, radishes, and dill marinade. Refrigerate for 1 hour.

Spray grill rack with nonflammable cooking spray. Preheat grill to medium-high heat (350° to 400°).

Thread vegetables onto skewers. Sprinkle with salt and pepper. Grill vegetables, covered, turning at least twice, for about 15 minutes. Garnish with thyme, if desired.

CHICKEN AND ONION KABOBS

Chicken and onions take on the grill and can be topped with fresh herbs for a sophisticated look.

YIELD: 4 TO 6 SERVINGS

- 4 boneless skinless chicken breasts, cut into 2-inch pieces
- ½ (10-ounce) package purple pearl onions, blanched and peeled
- ½ (10-ounce) package white pearl onions, blanched and peeled
- 4 to 6 wooden skewers, soaked in water for 30 minutes
- ½ cup vegetable oil
- 1 teaspoon kosher salt
- ¾ teaspoon ground black pepper
- Garnish: fresh thyme

Spray grill rack with nonflammable cooking spray. Preheat grill to medium-high heat (350° to 400°).

Thread chicken and onions onto skewers. Brush kabobs with oil; sprinkle with salt and pepper.

Grill kabobs, covered, for 6 to 8 minutes. Garnish with thyme, if desired.

GRILLED CHICKEN QUESADILLAS

Fire up the grill and bring some Southwestern flair to your next cookout.

⸻⸺⸺⸺⸺⸺⸺⸺⸺⸺⸺

YIELD: 4 SERVINGS

4	fresh jalapeños, halved lengthwise and seeded
3	peaches, peeled, halved, and pitted
1	yellow onion, sliced ½ inch thick
4	cups chopped cooked chicken
4	cups shredded Monterey Jack cheese
2	green onions, chopped
3	tablespoons chopped fresh cilantro
1	tablespoon lime zest
1	tablespoon fresh lime juice
1	teaspoon kosher salt
4	(10-inch) flour tortillas

Grilled limes, to serve

Spray grill rack with nonflammable cooking spray. Preheat grill to high heat (400° to 450°).

Grill jalapeño, peaches, and onion, covered, for 3 to 5 minutes per side. Remove from grill, and let cool completely. Remove skin from jalapeño; discard. Finely chop jalapeño. Chop peach and onion.

In a large bowl, stir together jalapeño, peaches, onion, chicken, cheese, green onion, cilantro, lime zest and juice, and salt.

Divide mixture among tortillas, spreading on one half of each tortilla. Fold tortillas in half.

Grill over indirect heat, uncovered, until cheese is melted and both sides are golden brown, about 2 minutes per side. Serve with grilled limes.

GINGER-SPICED PORK CHOPS

The flavors of ginger and teriyaki in this marinade make these chops subtly sweet and spicy.

YIELD: 4 SERVINGS

1½ cups vegetable oil
¼   cup teriyaki sauce
¼   cup rice vinegar
1   tablespoon chopped fresh
    cilantro
1   tablespoon ground coriander
2   teaspoons grated fresh ginger
2½ teaspoons kosher salt, divided
2   teaspoons ground black
    pepper, divided
1   teaspoon ground cumin
4   (2-inch-thick) bone-in pork
    chops

In a small bowl, whisk together oil, teriyaki sauce, vinegar, cilantro, coriander, ginger, 1½ teaspoons salt, 1 teaspoon pepper, and cumin. Place marinade and pork chops in a resealable plastic bag. Seal bag; refrigerate for 4 hours.

Remove pork chops from bag; discard marinade. Let stand at room temperature for at least 30 minutes. Sprinkle pork chops with remaining 1 teaspoon salt and remaining 1 teaspoon pepper.

Spray grill rack with nonflammable cooking spray. Preheat grill to medium-high heat (350° to 400°).

Grill pork chops, covered, until a meat thermometer registers 145°, about 7 minutes per side.

GRILLED SESAME SALMON

This salmon's flavor profile makes it a hit for even the most discerning of palates.

YIELD: 4 TO 6 SERVINGS

½ cup sesame oil
½ cup sweet chipotle sauce
¼ cup honey
1½ teaspoons kosher salt, divided
1 teaspoon ground black pepper, divided
1 (2½-pound) side of salmon, pin bones removed
½ teaspoon white sesame seeds
½ teaspoon black sesame seeds
Garnish: sliced green onion, fresh chives, fresh cilantro, fresh dill, lime wedges

In a small bowl, whisk together oil, chipotle sauce, honey, ¾ teaspoon salt, and ½ teaspoon pepper. Reserve ⅓ cup marinade. Place salmon in a 13x9-inch baking dish. Pour remaining marinade over salmon. Cover with plastic wrap, and refrigerate for at least 8 hours or overnight.

Spray grill rack with nonflammable cooking spray. Preheat grill to medium-high heat (350° to 400°).

Remove salmon from refrigerator; discard marinade. Sprinkle salmon with sesame seeds. Grill, skin side down, for 7 to 10 minutes. Using a wide spatula, carefully turn fish. Grill until salmon reaches desired degree of doneness, 7 to 10 minutes more.

Transfer to a serving platter, skin side down. Garnish with green onion, chives, cilantro, dill, and lime wedges, if desired. Serve with reserved ⅓ cup marinade.

THE PERFECT BURGER

Why mess with perfection? This burger represents the simple goodness of Americana.
We'll leave the "Cheese or No Cheese" debate up to you.

YIELD: 8 SERVINGS

2½ pounds grass-fed ground
    beef (85% lean/15% fat)
3   teaspoons garlic salt
2   teaspoons ground black pepper
8   ounces Monterey Jack cheese,
    sliced
8   hamburger buns
Toppings: sliced tomatoes, lettuce,
    grilled red onion, cooked
    bacon slices

In a large bowl, gently combine beef, garlic salt, and pepper. Refrigerate, uncovered, for at least 2 hours.

Divide beef mixture into 8 portions, and gently shape each portion into a patty, about 1 inch thick.

Spray grill rack with nonflammable cooking spray. Preheat grill to medium-high heat (350° to 400°).

Place patties on grill; do not move for 2 minutes. Grill, uncovered, turning every 2 to 3 minutes, until burgers reach desired degree of doneness.

Reduce heat to medium (300° to 350°). Top patties with cheese; cover and grill until cheese is melted. Transfer to a platter, and let cool slightly. Serve burgers on buns with desired toppings.

PORK TENDERLOIN SANDWICHES

Homemade caramelized onion mayonnaise is what makes this sandwich special.
The apples, cheese, onions, and pork combo will be your new favorite.

YIELD: 8 SERVINGS

CARAMELIZED ONION MAYO

1 tablespoon canola oil
2 cups chopped yellow onion
¼ teaspoon salt
2 to 5 tablespoons water
1½ cups mayonnaise

PORK

2 (1-pound) pork tenderloins
1 tablespoon canola oil
1 teaspoon salt
½ teaspoon ground black pepper
1 cup whole-grain mustard
8 kaiser rolls, halved
8 slices Havarti cheese
2 Braeburn apples, cored and thinly sliced
4 cups fresh arugula

FOR MAYO: In a medium skillet, heat oil over medium-high heat. Add onion; cook, stirring occasionally, until lightly browned around edges, about 4 minutes. Reduce heat to medium-low. Sprinkle with salt; gradually stir in 2 tablespoons water. Cook, stirring occasionally, until deep golden brown, about 15 minutes. (Stir in additional water to prevent onion from sticking to pan, if needed.) Let stand until cool.

Spoon onion into a small bowl. Stir in mayonnaise until combined. Cover and refrigerate until ready to serve.

FOR PORK: Spray grill rack with nonflammable cooking spray. Preheat grill to medium-high heat (350° to 400°).

Drizzle pork with oil, and sprinkle with salt and pepper. Grill pork, covered, turning every 5 minutes, until a meat thermometer inserted in thickest portion registers 145°, 18 to 22 minutes. Let stand for 10 minutes; cut into ¼-inch slices.

Spread Caramelized Onion Mayo and mustard on rolls. Top with sliced pork, cheese, apple, and arugula.

BARBECUE-MARINATED PORK KABOBS

Who said barbecue sauce was only fit for shredded or sliced pork?

YIELD: APPROXIMATELY 5 SERVINGS

1   cup ketchup
¼   cup firmly packed light brown sugar
2   tablespoons apple cider vinegar
1   tablespoon Worcestershire sauce
1   teaspoon onion powder
1   teaspoon garlic powder
1   teaspoon ground black pepper
½   teaspoon crushed red pepper
3   pounds boneless country-style pork ribs, trimmed and cut into 2-inch pieces
Wooden skewers, soaked in water for 30 minutes

In a medium bowl, whisk together ketchup, brown sugar, vinegar, Worcestershire, onion powder, garlic powder, black pepper, and red pepper. Reserve ½ cup marinade. Place pork in a large resealable plastic bag; pour remaining marinade over pork. Seal bag; refrigerate for at least 8 hours.

Remove pork from bag; discard marinade. Let stand at room temperature for at least 30 minutes.

Spray grill rack with nonflammable cooking spray. Preheat grill to medium-high heat (350° to 400°).

Thread pork onto skewers. Grill over indirect heat, turning occasionally, until meat is cooked through, 20 to 25 minutes. Serve with reserved ½ cup marinade.

SAUSAGE DOGS WITH PEPPERS AND ONIONS

Spicy, snappy dogs simply scream summertime! Colorful bell peppers elevate this backyard classic and make for a beautiful presentation.

YIELD: 8 SERVINGS

2 tablespoons vegetable oil
4 cups (½-inch-thick) bell pepper strips (use a mix of colors)
2 cups (½-inch-thick) sliced onion
3 cloves garlic, minced
2 tablespoons red wine vinegar
2 teaspoons Creole seasoning
2 pounds smoked sausage,* cut as desired
8 hot dog buns
Whole-grain mustard, to serve

In a large skillet, heat oil over medium-high heat. Add peppers; cook until softened, 3 to 4 minutes. Add onion, garlic, vinegar, and Creole seasoning. Reduce heat to medium. Cover and cook until tender, 10 to 12 minutes.

Spray grill rack with nonflammable cooking spray. Preheat grill to medium-high heat (350° to 400°).

Grill sausage, covered, until grill marks form, 8 to 10 minutes, turning occasionally. Serve on buns with bell pepper mixture and mustard.

We used Conecuh.

BEER-MARINATED CHICKEN DRUMSTICKS

Sharing a brew with your bird makes for tasty drumsticks. Cheers!

YIELD: APPROXIMATELY 5 SERVINGS

2 tablespoons kosher salt
2 tablespoons firmly packed light brown sugar
2 tablespoons paprika
1 tablespoon ground black pepper
1 teaspoon ground red pepper
2 tablespoons olive oil
3 pounds chicken drumsticks
1 (12-ounce) can beer

In a large resealable plastic bag, combine salt, brown sugar, paprika, black pepper, and red pepper. Add oil and chicken. Seal bag, and shake until chicken is well coated. Pour beer into bag. Seal bag; refrigerate for at least 8 hours.

Remove chicken from bag; discard marinade. Let stand at room temperature for at least 30 minutes.

Spray grill rack with nonflammable cooking spray. Preheat grill to medium-high heat (350° to 400°).

Grill over indirect heat, covered, turning occasionally, until a meat thermometer inserted in thickest portion registers 160°, about 30 minutes.

BLACKENED GROUPER

Mild grouper is sophisticated with a little blackening. Grilled lemons are the perfect complement to top it all off.

YIELD: 4 TO 6 SERVINGS

¼   cup smoked paprika
2   tablespoons dried thyme
2   teaspoons onion powder
1½   teaspoons kosher salt
1½   teaspoons garlic powder
1   teaspoon ground black pepper
½   teaspoon dry mustard
½   teaspoon ground red pepper
½   cup butter, melted
2   pounds grouper fillets
1   tablespoon olive oil
3   lemons, halved

Preheat grill to high heat (400° to 450°). Preheat a 12-inch cast-iron skillet on grill for 15 minutes.

In a small bowl, stir together paprika, thyme, onion powder, salt, garlic powder, black pepper, mustard, and red pepper. Pour melted butter in a shallow dish. Dip each fillet in butter, turning to coat. Sprinkle both sides of fillets with spice mixture; pat gently to coat.

Add oil to skillet (oil should smoke); place fish in skillet. Grill, covered, until browned, 3 to 4 minutes. Turn, and grill, covered, until fish flakes easily with a fork, 3 to 4 minutes more. Carefully remove skillet from grill.

Place lemons cut side down on grill. Grill, covered, until charred, 3 to 4 minutes. Serve with fish.

GRILL-SMOKED CHICKEN

No smoker? No problem! Let your grill do double-duty and smoke some chickens tonight.

⸺ ⚓ ⸺

YIELD: APPROXIMATELY 8 SERVINGS

2   (4- to 5-pound) whole
    chickens, giblets discarded
Chicken Rub (recipe on page 23)
Alabama White Sauce (recipe on
    page 17)

Coat chickens with Chicken Rub. Tie legs together with kitchen twine. Wrap in plastic wrap, and refrigerate for at least 12 hours.

Prepare grill as directed on page 30; preheat grill to low (250° to 300°).

Place chicken on unlit side of grill. Grill, covered, until a meat thermometer inserted in thickest portion registers 165°, about 3 hours. Let stand for 10 minutes. Serve with Alabama White Sauce.

SKILLET STEAKS WITH GARLIC BROWNED BUTTER

Garlic browned butter made on the grill makes for melt in your mouth T-bone steaks.

YIELD: 4 TO 6 SERVINGS

2   teaspoons kosher salt
2   teaspoons ground black pepper
1   teaspoon garlic powder
2   (1½-inch-thick) T-bone steaks
1   tablespoon olive oil
3   tablespoons butter
2   cloves garlic, halved
Garnish: fresh oregano

Preheat grill to high heat (400° to 450°). Preheat a 12-inch cast-iron skillet on grill for 15 minutes.

In a small bowl, stir together salt, pepper, and garlic powder. Sprinkle both sides of steaks with spice mixture.

Add oil to skillet (oil should smoke); place steaks in skillet. Grill, uncovered, until browned, 3 to 4 minutes. Turn steaks; grill, covered, 4 minutes more. Uncover; add butter and garlic to skillet. Grill until butter is browned, 2 to 3 minutes. Carefully remove skillet from grill; spoon butter over steaks. Garnish with oregano, if desired.

CHICKEN UNDER A SKILLET

Whether you use another skillet or a foil-wrapped brick, this butterflied chicken will be sure to impress.

YIELD: 4 TO 6 SERVINGS

CHIPOTLE-LIME SAUCE

2   fresh jalapeños, halved and seeded
2   red chile peppers, halved and seeded
⅔   cup ketchup
⅔   cup orange juice
3   tablespoons fresh lime juice
2   tablespoons chopped fresh cilantro
¼   teaspoon ground chipotle chile powder

CHICKEN

¼   cup butter, softened
1   tablespoon chopped fresh cilantro
1   teaspoon lime zest
½   teaspoon garlic powder
¼   teaspoon kosher salt
¼   teaspoon ground black pepper
1   (4- to 5-pound) whole chicken, giblets and backbone removed

FOR CHIPOTLE-LIME SAUCE: Grill peppers, cut side up, covered, until blackened, 3 to 4 minutes. Place peppers in a resealable plastic bag. Seal bag; let stand for 15 minutes. Peel and discard skin from peppers.

In the container of a blender, combine peppers, ketchup, orange juice, lime juice, cilantro, and chile powder. Blend until smooth; set aside.

FOR CHICKEN: Spray grill rack with nonflammable cooking spray. Preheat grill to high heat (400° to 450°). Preheat a 12-inch cast-iron skillet on grill 15 minutes.

In a small bowl, stir together butter, cilantro, zest, garlic powder, salt, and pepper. Rub mixture under skin and on outside of chicken. Place chicken skin side down in skillet. Place a second skillet or a foil-wrapped brick over chicken.

Grill, covered, for 20 minutes. Remove top skillet; carefully turn chicken. Place skillet over chicken, and grill, covered, until a meat thermometer registers 165°, about 20 minutes more. Carefully remove skillet from grill. Serve with chipotle-lime sauce.

LEMON-HERB MARINATED FLANK STEAK

Citrus isn't just for fish—Flank steak gets a makeover with this citrusy herb marinade.

———————————⚹———————————

YIELD: APPROXIMATELY 5 SERVINGS

1   cup olive oil
½   cup fresh lemon juice
4   teaspoons kosher salt, divided
1   teaspoon crushed red pepper
1   cup chopped fresh parsley
1   cup chopped fresh basil
6   cloves garlic, sliced
1   (2½-pound) flank steak
1   teaspoon ground black pepper
Sliced zucchini, sliced red onion,
    cherry tomatoes, to serve
Garnish: fresh parsley, fresh basil

In a medium bowl, stir together oil, lemon juice, 2 teaspoons salt, and red pepper. Add parsley, basil, and garlic. Reserve ½ cup marinade.

Place steak in a large resealable plastic bag; pour remaining marinade over steak. Seal bag; refrigerate for at least 8 hours.

Remove steak from bag; discard marinade. Let stand at room temperature for at least 30 minutes. Sprinkle steak with black pepper and remaining 2 teaspoons salt.

Spray grill rack with nonflammable cooking spray. Preheat grill to medium-high heat (350° to 400°).

Grill steak, covered, turning occasionally, until desired degree of doneness is reached, about 8 minutes per side for medium. Remove from grill, and let stand for at least 5 minutes. Grill zucchini, red onion, and tomatoes over direct heat until grill marks form, about 5 minutes (use skewers, if desired).

To serve, thinly slice steak across the grain. Drizzle with reserved ½ cup marinade. Serve with grilled zucchini, red onion, and tomato. Garnish with parsley and basil, if desired.

CHAPTER THREE

Starters

APPETIZERS AND COCKTAILS FOR YOUR NEXT BARBECUE

OYSTER ROAST

Roll your sleeves up and get ready to shuck some oysters!
Served with three dipping sauces, there's something for everyone's personal tastes.

————————————— ⚓ —————————————

YIELD: 6 TO 8 SERVINGS

SPICY COCKTAIL SAUCE

½   cup ketchup
¼   cup hot sauce
2   tablespoons prepared
     horseradish, drained
1   teaspoon fresh lemon juice
1   teaspoon chopped fresh
     parsley

GARLIC-BUTTER SAUCE

½   cup unsalted butter
2   cloves garlic, minced
2   tablespoons chopped shallot
1   tablespoon fresh lemon juice
1   teaspoon kosher salt
1   teaspoon chopped fresh thyme

TARRAGON-BLACK PEPPER SAUCE

⅓   cup mayonnaise
¼   cup sour cream
2   tablespoons white wine vinegar
1   tablespoon chopped fresh
     tarragon
1   teaspoon kosher salt
1   teaspoon ground black pepper

OYSTERS

6   lemons, halved
48   fresh oysters

FOR SPICY COCKTAIL SAUCE: In a small bowl, combine ketchup, hot sauce, horseradish, lemon juice, and parsley. Cover and refrigerate for up to 1 week.

FOR GARLIC-BUTTER SAUCE: In a small saucepan, melt butter over medium heat; stir in garlic and shallot. Cook until soft and translucent, approximately 1 minute; stir in lemon juice, salt, and thyme. Keep warm until serving, or cover and refrigerate for up to 3 days. Warm before serving.

FOR TARRAGON-BLACK PEPPER SAUCE: In a small bowl, combine mayonnaise, sour cream, vinegar, tarragon, salt, and pepper. Cover and refrigerate for up to 3 days.

FOR OYSTERS: Preheat grill to high heat (400° to 450°).

Place lemons, cut side down, on grill, and cook until browned, approximately 2 minutes.

Place oysters on grill, and cook until shells barely open, approximately 10 minutes. Remove from grill; shuck using a towel or silicone oven mitt. Oysters will be very hot. Serve with Spicy Cocktail Sauce, Garlic-Butter Sauce, Tarragon-Black Pepper Sauce, and grilled lemons.

SPICY CORN DIP WITH BACON AND SMOKED CHEDDAR

Crispy grilled tortilla chips have the pleasure of being dipped, dunked, and scooped into this cheesy corn dip that doesn't quit. Ground red pepper and hot sauce give this dip a fiery kick, but if that's not your style — adjust their measurements to your preference.

YIELD: APPROXIMATELY 6 SERVINGS

GRILLED TORTILLAS
- 20 (6-inch) corn tortillas
- ½ cup canola oil
- 5 teaspoons salt
- 5 teaspoons ground black pepper
- 5 teaspoons chili powder

CORN DIP
- 4 ounces cream cheese, softened
- 2 cups shredded smoked Cheddar cheese
- 1 cup fresh corn kernels (from approximately 2 ears corn)
- ¼ cup sour cream
- ¼ cup barbecue sauce
- 1 teaspoon Worcestershire sauce
- ½ teaspoon hot sauce
- ½ teaspoon ground red pepper
- 4 slices bacon, cooked and crumbled

FOR GRILLED TORTILLAS: Spray grill rack with nonflammable cooking spray. Preheat grill to medium heat (300° to 350°).

Place tortillas in a single layer on a baking sheet. Brush both sides with oil; sprinkle with salt, pepper, and chili powder.

Grill tortillas until grill marks form and tortillas are crisp, approximately 2 minutes per side; let cool. Break into pieces, if desired.

FOR CORN DIP: In a medium bowl, stir together cream cheese, Cheddar, corn, sour cream, barbecue sauce, Worcestershire, hot sauce, red pepper, and bacon. Serve with Grilled Tortillas.

SIPS TO SHARE

GINGERY PEACH SHANDY

GINGERY PEACH SHANDY

Beat the heat with this spicy and sweet twist on the original beer cocktail.

YIELD: 6 SERVINGS

4   (12-ounce) bottles chilled ginger beer
2   (12-ounce) bottles chilled lager beer
2   tablespoons fresh lime juice
2   tablespoons fresh lemon juice
Garnish: peach slices, lemon slices, lime slices, fresh mint sprigs

In a small pitcher, combine ginger beer, beer, lime juice, and lemon juice. Serve immediately over ice. Garnish with peach slices, lemon slices, lime slices, and mint, if desired.

PALE ALE BLACKBERRY DELIGHT

This frothy beer cocktail is sure to help quench your thirst.

YIELD: 6 TO 8 SERVINGS

3   cups fresh blackberries, divided
1   tablespoon honey
1   teaspoon grated fresh ginger
¾   cup cold honey bourbon*
1   bunch fresh mint leaves, torn
6   (12-ounce) bottles cold pale ale

In the container of a blender, place 1 cup blackberries, honey, and ginger. Process until smooth.

In a large pitcher, place bourbon, mint, and remaining 2 cups blackberries. Muddle until blackberries are crushed. Pour blackberry purée over muddled fruit. Slowly add pale ale, tilting pitcher to reduce foam. Stir until combined. Serve immediately.

We used Jack Daniel's Honey Bourbon.

PALE ALE BLACKBERRY
DELIGHT AND LAGER REFRESHER

LAGER REFRESHER

Citrus juices, gin, and beer come together to create an easy-drinking summer cocktail.

YIELD: 6 TO 8 SERVINGS

¾   cup cold gin
½   cup fresh lime juice
½   cup fresh orange juice
4   limes, thinly sliced
2   oranges, thinly sliced
6   (12-ounce) bottles cold lager beer

In a large pitcher, combine gin, lime juice, orange juice, lime slices, and orange slices. Slowly add lager, tilting pitcher to reduce foam. Stir until combined. Serve immediately.

WATERMELON LEMONADE

WATERMELON LEMONADE

This tart lemonade is smoothed out with refreshing watermelon juice that hits just the right note of sweetness.

YIELD: APPROXIMATELY 2 QUARTS

½ cup sugar
½ cup water
10 cups cubed seedless watermelon
½ small seedless watermelon, cut into wedges
2 lemons, sliced
1½ cups fresh lemon juice
Garnish: watermelon wedges, lemon slices

In a small saucepan, bring sugar and ½ cup water to a boil, stirring until sugar is dissolved. Remove from heat; let cool completely.

In the container of a blender, place half of cubed watermelon; process until smooth. Press juice through a fine-mesh sieve into a large bowl, discarding solids. Repeat procedure with remaining cubed watermelon, reserving 6 cups juice.

In a large pitcher, place watermelon wedges and lemon slices. Add sugar mixture, reserved watermelon juice, and lemon juice; stir gently. Serve over ice. Garnish with watermelon wedges and lemon slices, if desired.

SPICED RUM PUNCH

Bring the taste of the Caribbean to your next barbecue with this bubbly punch.

YIELD: APPROXIMATELY 8 SERVINGS

1 cup fresh orange juice
2 sticks cinnamon
4 whole cloves
16 ounces pineapple juice
8 ounces spiced rum
2 (5.5-ounce) cans Kern's peach nectar
4 cups club soda
Garnish: orange slices

In a saucepan, bring orange juice, cinnamon, and cloves to a boil. Remove from heat, and let cool completely.

Strain orange juice mixture into a large pitcher, and discard solids. Add pineapple juice, rum, and peach nectar. Refrigerate for at least 2 hours or up to 3 days. Add club soda, and serve over ice. Garnish with orange slices, if desired.

SPICED RUM PUNCH

ROSEMARY-LEMON SHRIMP SKEWERS

Fresh shrimp are immersed in aromatic, floral rosemary in this dish.
Using the herb sprigs as skewers makes a beautiful finished product.

YIELD: 6 SERVINGS

½   cup olive oil
2   tablespoons chopped fresh
    rosemary
1   tablespoon lemon zest
1½ teaspoons kosher salt
1   teaspoon ground black pepper
1½ pounds peeled and deveined
    extra-jumbo fresh shrimp (tails
    left on)
18 (8- to 10-inch) sprigs fresh
    rosemary
2   lemons, cut into wedges
2   medium zucchini, sliced
    2 inches thick

In a small bowl, combine oil, rosemary, zest, salt, and pepper, whisking to combine. Add shrimp, tossing to coat. Cover and refrigerate for 1 hour.

Spray grill rack with nonflammable cooking spray. Preheat grill to medium-high heat (350° to 400°).

Strip rosemary leaves from stems, leaving 2 to 3 inches with leaves remaining at the ends. Reserve remaining leaves for another use. Skewer shrimp onto rosemary sprigs alternating with lemon and zucchini slices. Grill skewers for 2 minutes. Turn skewers, and grill until shrimp are pink and firm, approximately 2 minutes more.

GRILLED BRIE WITH PEACHES

This French cheese gets the Southern treatment with juicy peaches and sweet honey.

YIELD: APPROXIMATELY 10 SERVINGS

¾ cup honey
3 tablespoons fresh lemon juice
3 peaches, pitted and halved
2 (4-ounce) rounds Brie cheese
1 (15x6-inch) cedar plank, soaked
   in water for 1 hour
Crackers, to serve
Garnish: fresh mint

Spray grill rack with nonflammable cooking spray. Preheat grill to medium heat (300° to 350°).

In a small bowl, whisk together honey and lemon juice. Brush peaches and cheese with honey mixture.

Grill cheese, uncovered, for 3 minutes. Transfer to prepared plank, and grill, covered, 15 minutes more. Remove plank from grill.

Grill peaches, cut side down, covered, for 5 minutes. Turn peaches over; brush with honey mixture. Grill 5 minutes more.

Serve cheese with peaches and crackers. Garnish with mint, if desired.

CRISPY BACON DEVILED EGGS

Enjoy this dish with a dash of salty bacon and sweet pickle relish to take these eggs up a notch. It may not have devilish qualities, but it sure does taste sinful.

YIELD: 12 SERVINGS

4	slices bacon, chopped	1	tablespoon Dijon mustard
6	hard-cooked eggs, peeled and halved lengthwise	1	tablespoon sweet pickle relish
¼	cup mayonnaise	½	teaspoon garlic salt
		¼	cup sliced green onion

In a medium skillet, cook bacon over medium heat until crisp. Remove from pan using a slotted spoon, and let drain on paper towels, reserving drippings in pan.

Scoop egg yolks into a medium bowl, and mash with a fork. Stir in reserved drippings, mayonnaise, mustard, relish, and garlic salt. Fold in green onion and half of chopped bacon.

Scoop yolk mixture into center of each egg white. Garnish with remaining chopped bacon, if desired.

CHILLED CORN SOUP WITH CUCUMBER RELISH

Soup in the summer heat may not sound ideal, but this chilled corn soup will make you a believer.

YIELD: APPROXIMATELY 6 SERVINGS

4 large fresh thyme sprigs
1 bay leaf
Butcher's twine
1 tablespoon canola oil, plus more for grilling
½ cup chopped shallot
1 clove garlic, minced
6 cups fresh corn kernels (from 6 to 8 ears corn)
1½ cups water
1½ cups chicken broth
1¼ teaspoons kosher salt
¼ teaspoon ground red pepper
6 large fresh shrimp, peeled and deveined (tails left on)
⅛ teaspoon salt, plus more to taste
Ground black pepper, to taste
½ cup chopped seedless cucumber
¼ cup chopped tomato
1 tablespoon red wine vinegar
1 tablespoon chopped fresh chives

Tie thyme and bay leaf together with butcher's twine. Set aside.

In a large saucepan, heat oil over medium heat. Add shallot and garlic; cook until lightly browned, 4 to 5 minutes. Add corn, 1½ cups water, broth, salt, red pepper, and thyme bundle. Bring to a boil over medium-high heat; reduce heat, and simmer for 5 minutes. Remove from heat, and let cool slightly. Discard thyme bundle.

With an immersion blender, blend until smooth. Strain corn mixture through a fine-mesh sieve, stirring and pressing with a spatula until thoroughly strained; discard solids. Cover and refrigerate until chilled.

Brush a grill pan with oil, and heat over medium-high heat. Sprinkle shrimp with salt and pepper. Place in pan, and cook until pink and firm, approximately 2 minutes.

In a small bowl, toss together cucumber, tomato, vinegar, chives, and a pinch salt. Divide soup among 6 bowls, and serve with shrimp and tomato mixture.

GRILLED OKRA

Every now and again, it's good to remember okra doesn't have to be fried. With two dipping sauces, these won't last long!

YIELD: APPROXIMATELY 8 SERVINGS

ROASTED POBLANO DIP
- 1 large fresh poblano, halved lengthwise, seeds and membrane removed
- 1 cup plain Greek yogurt
- 2 tablespoons chopped fresh cilantro
- 2 tablespoons chopped fresh chives
- 2 teaspoons minced garlic
- ½ teaspoon kosher salt
- ½ teaspoon ground black pepper
- ½ teaspoon Cajun seasoning

SUMMER HERB RICOTTA DIP
- 1 cup ricotta cheese
- ½ cup sour cream
- 2 tablespoons minced shallot
- 2 tablespoons chopped fresh basil
- 2 tablespoons chopped fresh dill
- ½ teaspoon kosher salt
- ½ teaspoon ground black pepper

OKRA
- 2 pounds fresh okra
- 1 (16-ounce) jar cocktail onions, drained
- ¼ cup olive oil
- 1 teaspoon kosher salt
- 1 teaspoon ground black pepper
- 12 wooden skewers, soaked in water for 30 minutes

FOR ROASTED POBLANO DIP: Preheat oven to broil. Line a rimmed baking sheet with foil.

Place pepper, skin side up, on prepared pan. Broil until blackened, approximately 12 minutes. Place pepper in a bowl, and cover tightly with plastic wrap. Let stand until cool enough to handle, 10 to 15 minutes. Peel and discard skin from pepper, and chop finely.

In a small bowl, stir together chopped pepper, yogurt, cilantro, chives, garlic, salt, pepper, and Cajun seasoning. Cover and refrigerate for at least 2 hours before serving. Cover and refrigerate for up to 3 days.

SUMMER HERB RICOTTA DIP: In a small bowl, stir together ricotta, sour cream, shallot, basil, dill, salt, and pepper. Cover and refrigerate for at least 2 hours before serving. Cover and refrigerate for up to 3 days.

FOR OKRA: Spray grill rack with nonflammable cooking spray. Preheat grill to high heat (400° to 450°).

In a large bowl, combine okra, onions, oil, salt, and pepper, tossing to coat. Thread okra and onions onto skewers.

Grill okra, covered, until tender, 2 to 3 minutes per side. Remove from grill, and let cool slightly. Serve warm with Roasted Poblano Dip and Summer Herb Ricotta Dip.

OKRA AND CORN FRITTERS

These bite-sized nuggets of crunchy, sweet corn and okra won't last long on the table.

———————— ✤ ————————

YIELD: APPROXIMATELY 36

HERB-PEPPER CANE SYRUP
1   cup cane syrup*
2   tablespoons minced shallot
1   tablespoon ground black pepper
2   teaspoons chopped fresh rosemary
1   teaspoon kosher salt

FRITTERS
Peanut oil, for frying
5   cups self-rising buttermilk cornmeal mix
1   pound fresh okra, finely chopped
4   ears fresh corn, kernels removed from cob
2   teaspoons garlic powder
1   teaspoon salt
1   teaspoon ground black pepper
3   cups whole milk
2   large eggs, lightly beaten

FOR HERB-PEPPER CANE SYRUP: In a saucepan, bring cane syrup, shallot, pepper, rosemary, and salt to a boil over medium heat. Remove from heat, and let cool to room temperature.

FOR FRITTERS: In a large Dutch oven, pour oil to a depth of 4 inches, and heat over medium heat until a deep-fry thermometer registers 350°.

In a medium bowl, combine cornmeal mix, okra, corn, garlic powder, salt, and pepper, stirring to combine. In a small bowl, whisk together milk and eggs. Add milk mixture to cornmeal mixture, stirring to combine.

Drop batter in batches by rounded tablespoons into hot oil. Fry until golden brown, 5 to 6 minutes. Let drain on paper towels. Serve warm with Herb-Pepper Cane Syrup.

We used Steen's.

QUICK-PICKLED OKRA

Though its water content isn't quite as high as a cucumber, okra is still mostly made of water, which results in a similar crunch to the traditional pickled snack food.

YIELD: 10 TO 12 SERVINGS

1 pound fresh okra, halved lengthwise
5 teaspoons salt, divided
½ yellow onion, thinly sliced
5 to 6 dried chile peppers
4 cloves garlic
3 cups water
1½ cups distilled white vinegar
2 teaspoons sugar
2 tablespoons mixed peppercorns

Place okra in a colander; sprinkle with 2 teaspoons salt, and let stand for 15 minutes. Rinse okra thoroughly to remove slimy residue.

In a large nonreactive heatproof bowl, place okra, onion, chiles, and garlic.

In a large nonreactive saucepan, bring 3 cups water and vinegar to a boil over high heat. Add sugar and remaining 3 teaspoons salt, stirring until dissolved. Add peppercorns, stirring well.

Pour hot vinegar mixture over okra. Let cool at room temperature for 1 hour.

Place a plate on top of okra to keep it submerged; refrigerate for at least 4 hours before serving. Store in an airtight container in the refrigerator for up to 5 days.

PIMIENTO CHEESE

Spread it on crackers, put it between two slices of bread, or eat it with a spoon. This Southern delicacy is a favorite every year at The Masters, as well as backyards throughout the Southeast.

YIELD: APPROXIMATELY 8 SERVINGS

2   (4-ounce) blocks extra-sharp Cheddar cheese, shredded
2   (4-ounce) jars diced pimientos, drained
2/3 cup mayonnaise
1   teaspoon smoked paprika
1   teaspoon hot sauce
1/2 teaspoon kosher salt
1/4 teaspoon ground black pepper
1   baguette, sliced
1/4 cup canola oil
Sliced pickles, to serve

In a large bowl, stir together cheese, pimientos, mayonnaise, paprika, hot sauce, salt, and pepper. Cover and refrigerate for at least 30 minutes or up to 2 days.

Heat a grill pan over medium-high heat. Lightly brush bread with oil, and place on grill pan. Cook until grill marks form, approximately 1 minute per side. Serve Pimiento Cheese with grilled bread and pickles.

SMOKED CRAB DIP

Easy and elegant, this smoked crab dip with freshly toasted baguette rounds is sure to be a crowd-pleaser.

---✦---

YIELD: 6 TO 8 SERVINGS

HERBED BAGUETTE ROUNDS

1	French baguette, sliced into ¼-inch rounds
½	cup unsalted butter, melted
2	tablespoons chopped fresh parsley
1	tablespoon chopped fresh chives
½	teaspoon Cajun seasoning

CRAB DIP

2	(8-ounce) packages whipped cream cheese, softened
1	cup plain Greek yogurt
3	tablespoons chopped green onion
2	tablespoons minced shallot
1	tablespoon Creole seasoning
1	tablespoon grated fresh horseradish
1	tablespoon Worcestershire sauce
2	teaspoons fresh lemon juice
2	teaspoons liquid smoke
1	teaspoon minced fresh garlic
1	teaspoon ground black pepper
1	(8-ounce) container crab claw meat, picked free of shell
1	(8-ounce) container jumbo lump crabmeat, picked free of shell

FOR HERBED BAGUETTE ROUNDS: Preheat oven to 350°. Line a baking sheet with foil.

Lightly brush bread slices with melted butter. In a small bowl, combine parsley, chives, and Cajun seasoning; sprinkle over bread slices.

Bake until toasted, approximately 12 minutes. Remove from oven, and let cool completely.

FOR CRAB DIP: In a large bowl, beat cream cheese and yogurt with a mixer at medium-high speed until smooth and creamy, approximately 2 minutes.

Add onion, shallot, Creole seasoning, horseradish, and Worcestershire; beat at medium speed until combined. Add lemon juice, liquid smoke, garlic, and pepper, beating until combined. Using a spatula, fold crab into mixture. Serve with Herbed Baguette Rounds.

GRILLED SHRIMP
WITH TOMATILLO SALSA

Tomatillos may look like funny green tomatoes with a dry skin like an onion,
however, they are a different vegetable entirely, and can make a mean salsa.

YIELD: APPROXIMATELY 6 SERVINGS

TOMATILLO SALSA

1   pound tomatillos, husked and halved
3   tablespoons vegetable oil
1   cup fresh cilantro leaves
2   fresh jalapeños, stemmed, halved, and seeded
3   cloves garlic, peeled
3   tablespoons fresh lime juice
½   teaspoon salt
¼   teaspoon ground black pepper

GRILLED SHRIMP

2   pounds peeled and deveined colossal fresh shrimp (tails left on)
¼   cup extra-virgin olive oil
2   tablespoons minced garlic
1   tablespoon lime zest
1   teaspoon kosher salt
1   teaspoon crushed red pepper
½   teaspoon ground black pepper
Garnish: lime wedges, fresh cilantro

FOR TOMATILLO SALSA: Spray grill rack with nonflammable cooking spray. Preheat grill to medium-high heat (350° to 400°).

In a small bowl, stir together tomatillos and oil. Grill tomatillos, turning occasionally, until softened and slightly charred, approximately 5 minutes. Let cool completely.

In the work bowl of a food processor, pulse together tomatillos, cilantro, jalapeño, garlic, and lime juice until combined, 3 to 4 times. Stir in salt and pepper.

FOR GRILLED SHRIMP: In a large resealable plastic bag, combine shrimp, oil, garlic, zest, salt, red pepper, and black pepper. Seal bag; refrigerate for 1 hour.

Spray grill rack with nonflammable cooking spray. Preheat grill to medium-high heat (350° to 400°).

Remove shrimp from bag; discard marinade. Grill, covered, until pink and firm, 4 to 5 minutes per side. Remove from heat, and let cool slightly. Garnish with lime wedges and cilantro, if desired. Serve with Tomatillo Salsa.

GRILLED CORN SALSA

Southwestern flavors abound in this corn salsa. Black beans, bell peppers,
and fresh cilantro add different dimensions to this flavorful dish.

YIELD: 6 CUPS

6   ears fresh yellow corn
2   tablespoons vegetable oil
1½   teaspoons kosher salt, divided
1   teaspoon ground black pepper,
      divided
1   (14.5-ounce) can black beans,
      rinsed and drained
1   cup quartered grape tomatoes
½   cup chopped green bell pepper
⅓   cup fresh lime juice
¼   cup extra-virgin olive oil
2   tablespoons chopped fresh
      cilantro
2   tablespoons fresh lemon juice
¼   teaspoon smoked paprika
¼   teaspoon ground red pepper
Tortilla chips, to serve

Spray grill rack with nonflammable cooking spray. Preheat grill to
medium-high heat (350° to 400°).

Drizzle corn with vegetable oil, and sprinkle with ½ teaspoon salt and
½ teaspoon black pepper. Grill until charred, approximately 3 minutes per
side. Remove from heat. Let cool. Cut kernels from cob.

In a large bowl, combine corn kernels, beans, tomatoes, bell pepper,
lime juice, olive oil, cilantro, lemon juice, paprika, red pepper, remaining
1 teaspoon salt, and remaining ½ teaspoon black pepper. Cover and
refrigerate for at least 1 hour or up to 4 hours. Serve with tortilla chips.

CHAPTER FOUR

Sides

MADE FROM SCRATCH

GRILLED CABBAGE WEDGES

Cabbage's satisfying crunch makes it indispensable in coleslaw. In this simple salad, it's the star.

SPICY LIME DRESSING

1	cup sour cream
¼	teaspoon lime zest
1	tablespoon plus 1 teaspoon fresh lime juice
1	tablespoon water
¼	teaspoon smoked paprika
¼	teaspoon kosher salt
⅛	teaspoon ground red pepper

GRILLED CABBAGE

½	head red cabbage
½	head green cabbage
1	tablespoon canola oil
1	teaspoon kosher salt
¼	teaspoon ground black pepper

FOR DRESSING: In a small bowl, stir together sour cream, lime zest and juice, 1 tablespoon water, paprika, salt, and red pepper. Cover and refrigerate for up to 2 days.

FOR GRILLED CABBAGE: Spray grill rack with nonflammable cooking spray. Preheat grill to medium-high heat (350° to 400°).

Slice each half head of cabbage into 3 wedges. Brush wedges with oil, and sprinkle with salt and pepper. Grill cabbage, cut side down, until cabbage begins to char and soften, 6 to 8 minutes per side. Serve with Spicy Lime Dressing.

APPLE-JICAMA SLAW

Granny Smiths provide a snappy, tart flavor to the nutty jicama in this crunchy slaw.
Its bright green appearance will also be a delight for the eye on any table spread.

YIELD: 8 TO 10 SERVINGS

3	Granny Smith apples, cored and thinly sliced
½	pound jicama, thinly sliced
½	head green cabbage, thinly sliced
1	bunch radishes, sliced ⅛ inch thick
½	cup chopped fresh cilantro
½	cup extra-virgin olive oil
¼	cup fresh lemon juice
1	teaspoon Dijon mustard
1	teaspoon fine sea salt
½	teaspoon ground black pepper

In a large bowl, place apple, jicama, cabbage, and radish; toss to combine.

In a small bowl, whisk together cilantro, oil, lemon juice, mustard, salt, and pepper until combined, 20 to 30 seconds. Add dressing to apple mixture, and toss to coat. Serve immediately.

FRIED OKRA AND HEIRLOOM TOMATO SALAD

Different shapes and sizes of heirloom tomatoes are a festive backdrop to fried okra in this salad.

YIELD: APPROXIMATELY 4 SERVINGS

BUTTERMILK DRESSING
- ½ cup crème fraîche
- 3 tablespoons whole buttermilk
- 1 tablespoon chopped fresh chives
- 1 teaspoon lemon zest
- 2 teaspoons fresh lemon juice
- ¼ teaspoon sweet paprika
- ¼ teaspoon ground red pepper

FRIED OKRA
- 2 cups plain yellow cornmeal
- ½ cup all-purpose flour
- 4 teaspoons Creole seasoning
- 1 teaspoon kosher salt
- 1 teaspoon baking powder
- 1 teaspoon ground red pepper
- ½ teaspoon ground black pepper
- 1 cup whole buttermilk
- 1 large egg
- 1 teaspoon lemon zest
- Vegetable oil, for frying
- 1 pound okra, halved lengthwise

SALAD
- 4 large heirloom tomatoes, sliced ⅓ inch thick
- 3 medium heirloom tomatoes, sliced ⅓ inch thick
- 1 pint heirloom cherry or grape tomatoes, halved
- Garnish: chopped fresh chives

FOR DRESSING: In a small bowl, whisk together crème fraîche, buttermilk, chives, lemon zest and juice, paprika, and red pepper until combined. Cover and refrigerate for up to 3 days.

FOR OKRA: In a shallow bowl, whisk together cornmeal, flour, Creole seasoning, salt, baking powder, red pepper, and black pepper. In another shallow bowl, whisk together buttermilk, egg, and zest.

In a large skillet, pour oil to a depth of 2 inches, and heat over medium-high heat until a deep-fry thermometer registers 350°. Dip okra in buttermilk mixture, and dredge in cornmeal mixture, shaking off excess. Fry in batches until golden brown, approximately 2 minutes. Let drain on paper towels.

FOR SALAD: On a large platter, arrange tomatoes as desired. Top with Fried Okra, and drizzle with Buttermilk Dressing. Garnish with chives, if desired. Serve immediately.

GRILLED CAJUN CORN

Kick up corn on the cob to the max with some Cajun flavor.

YIELD: 6 SERVINGS

1 cup butter, softened
2 tablespoons chopped fresh dill
2 tablespoons chopped fresh basil
2 tablespoons chopped fresh chives
2 tablespoons chopped fresh parsley
¼ cup plus 1 tablespoon Cajun seasoning,* divided
8 ears fresh corn (in husks)
10 cups cold water
2 cups Cotija cheese
Garnish: fresh cilantro

In the work bowl of a food processor, place butter, dill, basil, chives, parsley, and 1 tablespoon Cajun seasoning; pulse until combined. Set aside.

Pull outer husks down ear of corn to the base, leaving intact. Remove silks, and fold husks back into place. Secure with kitchen twine. Fill a large bowl with 10 cups cold water, and add remaining ¼ cup Cajun seasoning. Add corn, and let soak for 10 minutes.

Spray grill rack with nonflammable cooking spray. Preheat grill to medium heat (300° to 350°).

Remove corn from water, shaking to remove excess water. Grill corn, covered, turning every 5 minutes, until kernels are tender, approximately 20 minutes.

Remove corn from grill, and let cool slightly. Pull back husks, and secure with kitchen twine, if desired. Spread approximately 2 tablespoons butter mixture on each ear of corn. Season with additional Cajun seasoning, if desired. Sprinkle each ear with approximately ¼ cup Cotija cheese. Garnish with cilantro, if desired.

We used Slap Ya Mama.

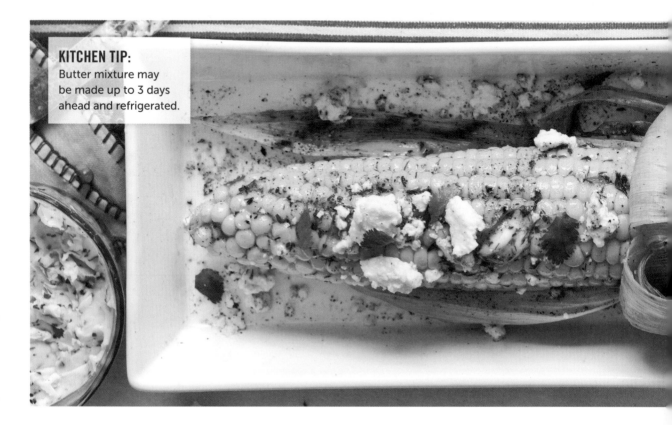

KITCHEN TIP:
Butter mixture may be made up to 3 days ahead and refrigerated.

PEPPER-PECAN SLAW

Creole mustard, toasted pecans, and jalapeños join forces to create
a complex slaw full of spicy, nutty notes and crunchy cabbage.

YIELD: 6 SERVINGS

5   cups thinly sliced green cabbage
½   cup thinly sliced red bell pepper
½   cup thinly sliced yellow bell pepper
2   banana peppers, seeded and cut into rings
1   small red or green fresh jalapeño, seeded and cut into rings
1   small poblano, seeded and thinly sliced
½   cup chopped fresh parsley
½   cup toasted pecans, chopped
½   cup mayonnaise
⅓   cup Creole mustard
2   tablespoons distilled white vinegar
½   teaspoon salt
1   teaspoon sugar

In a large bowl, combine cabbage, peppers, parsley, and pecans. In a small bowl, whisk together mayonnaise, mustard, vinegar, salt, and sugar. Pour over cabbage mixture; toss well. Cover and refrigerate for at least 1 hour or up to 6 hours.

TOMATO-WATERMELON SALAD WITH CANE SYRUP VINAIGRETTE

Fresh, juicy tomatoes and watermelon come together in this easy slice-and-serve salad.

YIELD: 6 TO 8 SERVINGS

½ small watermelon, chilled and cut into wedges

2½ pounds fresh tomatoes, cut into wedges

1 cup small fresh basil leaves

½ small red onion, thinly sliced

¼ cup red wine vinegar

2 tablespoons cane syrup

2 teaspoons canola oil

½ teaspoon kosher salt

½ teaspoon ground black pepper

On a large platter, arrange watermelon, tomatoes, basil, and red onion. In a small bowl, whisk together vinegar, cane syrup, and oil. Drizzle over salad. Sprinkle with salt and pepper. Serve immediately.

BORRACHO BEANS

Baked beans aren't the only belle of the barbecue. These pintos will have you second-guessing your go-to baked bean recipes.

YIELD: 8 TO 10 SERVINGS

1   (16-ounce) package dried pinto
    beans
6   cups chicken broth
1   (12-ounce) bottle beer
1   (14.5-ounce) can diced
    tomatoes
1   medium onion, chopped
1   clove garlic, minced
2   bay leaves
1   tablespoon chili powder
1   tablespoon salt
1   teaspoon garlic salt
1   teaspoon ground cumin
1   teaspoon dried oregano
Garnish: sliced onion, fresh cilantro

Rinse beans, and place in a large bowl. Cover with water, and let stand overnight. Drain.

In a large Dutch oven, bring beans, broth, beer, tomatoes, onion, garlic, bay leaves, chili powder, salt, garlic salt, cumin, and oregano to a boil over high heat. Reduce heat to medium-low; cover and simmer until beans are tender, approximately 1½ hours. Garnish with onion and cilantro, if desired.

CHOW CHOW

Two small words bring so much to the table in this side. So many flavors
come together to create a great alternative to sweet slaw.

YIELD: APPROXIMATELY 3 CUPS

¾   cup distilled white vinegar
⅔   cup sugar
¼   cup water
2   teaspoons salt
1   teaspoon mustard seeds
½   teaspoon ground turmeric
¼   teaspoon ground cloves
¼   teaspoon ground cinnamon

¼   teaspoon ground black pepper
1   medium fresh jalapeño, sliced
4   cups chopped green cabbage
1   cup fresh corn kernels
1   cup chopped white onion
1   cup diced red bell pepper
1   cup chopped seeded green tomato
½   cup chopped celery
1   garlic clove, minced

In a small Dutch oven, bring vinegar, sugar,
¼ cup water, salt, mustard seeds, turmeric,
cloves, cinnamon, black pepper, and jalapeño
to a boil over medium-high heat. Reduce heat
to medium-low; simmer for 2 minutes. Add
cabbage, corn, onion, bell pepper, tomato,
celery, and garlic; simmer for 20 minutes.
Remove from heat, and let cool completely.
Store in airtight containers in the refrigerator
for up to 3 weeks.

BRAISED COLLARD GREENS WITH COUNTRY HAM

This classic combo is always a good idea to have on hand at family get-togethers or backyard cookouts.

⚜

YIELD: 8 TO 10 SERVINGS

1 tablespoon canola oil
1 (4-ounce) slice country ham, chopped
2 cloves garlic, minced
2 cups chicken broth
⅓ cup apple cider vinegar
2 (16-ounce) packages chopped fresh collard greens
1 tablespoon sugar
2 teaspoons salt
1 teaspoon ground black pepper

In a large Dutch oven, heat oil over medium-high heat. Add ham; cook, stirring occasionally, until crisp, approximately 4 minutes. Add garlic, and cook for 1 minute. Add broth and vinegar, and cook for 2 to 3 minutes, scraping browned bits from bottom of pan with a wooden spoon. Stir in greens and sugar. Cover and simmer until greens are tender, approximately 30 minutes. Stir in salt and pepper.

GRILLED CORN SALAD

Colorful corn, red pepper, tomato, and cucumber come together with
smooth avocado and a vinaigrette that brings some heat.

YIELD: APPROXIMATELY 6 SERVINGS

SPICY CILANTRO VINAIGRETTE

- ¾ cup avocado oil
- ¼ cup Champagne vinegar
- ¼ cup chopped fresh cilantro
- 2 tablespoons minced fresh jalapeño
- 2 tablespoons minced shallot
- 2 teaspoons minced garlic
- 1 teaspoon salt
- ½ teaspoon ground black pepper

SALAD

- 6 ears fresh corn
- ⅓ cup vegetable oil
- 1¾ teaspoons kosher salt, divided
- 1 teaspoon ground black pepper, divided
- 1 cup roasted red peppers, drained and chopped
- 2 cups heirloom cherry tomatoes, halved
- 2 English cucumbers, peeled, seeded, and sliced
- 2 avocados, peeled, pitted, and diced
- 2 tablespoons fresh lemon juice

Garnish: fresh cilantro

FOR VINAIGRETTE: In a medium bowl, whisk together avocado oil and vinegar. Add cilantro, jalapeño, shallot, garlic, salt, and pepper, stirring to combine. Refrigerate for at least 2 hours.

FOR SALAD: Spray grill rack with nonflammable cooking spray. Preheat grill to medium-high heat (350° to 400°).

Brush corn with oil, and sprinkle with 1 teaspoon salt and ½ teaspoon pepper. Grill, turning at least twice, until lightly charred, approximately 15 minutes. Let cool completely. Cut corn kernels from cobs.

In a large bowl, combine corn, red pepper, tomatoes, and cucumbers. In a small bowl, gently toss together avocado and lemon juice; add to corn mixture. Add Spicy Cilantro Vinaigrette, remaining ¾ teaspoon salt, and remaining ½ teaspoon pepper, stirring gently to combine. Garnish with cilantro, if desired.

CORNMEAL-CRUSTED FRIED PICKLES

Dunk these fried pickles into barbecue sauce and enjoy the
extreme flavors of garlic and dill with hearty cornmeal.

YIELD: APPROXIMATELY 8 SERVINGS

Canola oil, for frying
1   cup whole buttermilk
1½   cups plain yellow cornmeal
½   cup all-purpose flour
2   teaspoons kosher salt, divided
4   cups garlic dill pickle slices*
Barbecue sauce, to serve

In a small Dutch oven, pour oil to halfway full, and heat over medium-high heat until a deep-fry thermometer registers 350°.

In a medium bowl, place buttermilk. In a shallow dish, stir together cornmeal, flour, and 1 teaspoon salt. Working in batches, dip pickle slices in buttermilk; dredge in cornmeal mixture, tossing gently to coat.

Fry in batches until golden brown, 2 to 3 minutes. (Adjust heat as needed to maintain 350°.) Let drain on paper towels. Sprinkle with remaining 1 teaspoon salt. Serve with barbecue sauce.

*We used Wickles.

CREAMY MUSTARD-DILL SLAW

Green and red cabbage swim in a spicy brown mustard sauce made creamy by mayonnaise.

YIELD: APPROXIMATELY 8 SERVINGS

7   cups thinly sliced green cabbage
1   cup thinly sliced red cabbage
½   cup shredded carrot
2   tablespoons sliced green onion
1   cup mayonnaise
2   tablespoons spicy brown
    mustard
2   tablespoons distilled white
    vinegar
1   tablespoon chopped fresh dill
1   teaspoon salt
½   teaspoon ground black pepper
Garnish: chopped fresh dill

In a large bowl, combine cabbage, carrot, and green onion. In a small bowl, stir together mayonnaise, mustard, vinegar, dill, salt, and pepper. Drizzle over cabbage mixture; toss to combine. Cover and refrigerate for at least 1 hour. Garnish with dill, if desired.

SLOW COOKER BOILED PEANUTS

Make this roadside staple in your own kitchen with a slow cooker and a bit of patience.

YIELD: 10 TO 12 SERVINGS

1   pound raw peanuts
1   cup salt, divided
1   gallon water
12 cups hot water
3   cloves garlic, smashed
1   bunch fresh dill, chopped
1   bunch fresh chives, chopped
4   (1-ounce) envelopes ranch dip
    mix
Garnish: fresh dill, fresh chives

Place peanuts in a large container. Add ½ cup salt and 1 gallon water; stir to combine. Place a dinner plate on top to weigh down peanuts. Soak for at least 8 hours or overnight. Drain; discard water.

In a 6-quart or larger slow cooker, combine soaked peanuts and remaining ½ cup salt. Add 12 cups hot water, stirring until salt is dissolved. Stir in garlic, dill, and chives. Cover and cook on high for 8 hours.

Stir in ranch dip mix; cover and cook until peanuts are tender, approximately 6 hours more. (Add hot water as needed to keep peanuts covered.) Remove peanuts from liquid. Garnish with dill and chives, if desired. Serve hot or cold. Cover and refrigerate for up to 1 week.

PURPLE HULL PEAS

Southern comfort flavors come together in this purple hull pea dish. Sausage, peas, okra, and tomatoes are simmered to perfection and served with cornbread.

YIELD: 6 TO 8 SERVINGS

2   tablespoons olive oil, divided
½   pound andouille sausage, sliced ¼ inch thick
½   cup chopped green bell pepper
¼   cup chopped celery
3   cups shelled fresh purple hull peas
1   pound plum tomatoes, peeled and chopped
1   cup sliced fresh okra
1   cup chicken broth
½   teaspoon salt
½   teaspoon ground cumin
¼   teaspoon ground red pepper
Cornbread, to serve

In a Dutch oven, heat 1 tablespoon oil over medium-high heat. Add sausage, bell pepper, and celery; cook for 3 to 4 minutes, stirring occasionally. Reduce heat to medium-low; add peas, tomatoes, okra, broth, salt, cumin, and red pepper. Cover and cook until peas are very tender, 20 to 30 minutes. Serve with cornbread.

FOUR-POTATO SALAD

Take your basic potato salad to the next level. These colorful potatoes add visual interest and a variety of textures.

---⚘---

YIELD: 8 TO 10 SERVINGS

1 pound sweet potatoes, peeled, sliced ¾ inch thick, and quartered

1 pound Yukon gold potatoes, sliced ¾ inch thick and quartered

1 pound red potatoes, halved

1¼ cups extra-virgin olive oil, divided

4½ teaspoons coarse sea salt, divided

1½ teaspoons ground black pepper, divided

1 pound purple potatoes, sliced ⅛ inch thick

¼ cup chopped fresh parsley

3 tablespoons apple cider vinegar

2 tablespoons whole-grain mustard

1½ teaspoons honey

Preheat oven to 375°. Line 2 rimmed baking sheets with foil.

On one prepared pan, place sweet potatoes, Yukon gold potatoes, and red potatoes. Drizzle with ½ cup plus 2 tablespoons oil, and sprinkle with 3 teaspoons salt and 1 teaspoon pepper. Mix with hands to evenly distribute.

Bake until potatoes are fork-tender, 16 to 18 minutes. Set aside, and let cool.

On remaining prepared pan, spread purple potatoes. Drizzle with 2 tablespoons oil, and sprinkle with remaining 1½ teaspoons salt and remaining ½ teaspoon pepper. Mix with hands to evenly distribute.

Bake until potatoes are fork-tender, 7 to 9 minutes. Set aside, and let cool.

In a large bowl, combine all potatoes. In a medium bowl, whisk together parsley, vinegar, mustard, honey, and remaining ½ cup oil. Pour over potatoes, tossing to combine.

ULTIMATE FRIED GREEN TOMATOES

Bacon, buttermilk, and a dash of Sriracha create a cool, yet savory sauce
that complements a stack of fresh-out-of-the-fryer green tomatoes.

YIELD: APPROXIMATELY 4 SERVINGS

BACON-BUTTERMILK DRESSING
4   slices bacon
½   cup mayonnaise
¼   cup whole buttermilk
1   tablespoon chopped fresh parsley
1   tablespoon chopped fresh chives
1   teaspoon whole-grain mustard
1   teaspoon Sriracha sauce
¼   teaspoon salt
¼   teaspoon ground black pepper

TOMATOES
16   (½-inch-thick) slices green tomato (approximately 1½ pounds)
3   teaspoons kosher salt, divided
1   cup whole buttermilk
2   teaspoons Sriracha sauce
1½   cups plain yellow cornmeal
1½   cups all-purpose flour
½   teaspoon ground black pepper
Vegetable oil, for frying
Garnish: salt, pepper

FOR BACON-BUTTERMILK DRESSING: In a medium skillet, cook bacon over medium heat until crisp. Remove bacon, and let drain on paper towels, reserving 1½ tablespoons drippings. Reserve bacon for garnish.

Spoon reserved 1½ tablespoons drippings into a medium bowl. Stir in mayonnaise, buttermilk, parsley, chives, mustard, Sriracha sauce, salt, and pepper. Cover and refrigerate until ready to serve.

FOR TOMATOES: Line a rimmed baking sheet with several layers of paper towels; top with a wire rack.

Place tomato slices on prepared rack. Sprinkle with 1 teaspoon salt. Let stand for 30 minutes. Pat tomato slices dry with paper towels.

In a shallow dish, whisk together buttermilk and Sriracha sauce. In another shallow dish, stir together cornmeal, flour, pepper, and remaining 2 teaspoons salt. Dip each tomato slice in buttermilk mixture, letting excess drip off. Dredge in cornmeal mixture, gently pressing mixture to tomatoes. Return tomatoes to prepared rack.

In a large Dutch oven, pour oil to halfway full, and heat over medium-high heat until a deep-fry thermometer registers 360°. Working in batches, carefully place tomatoes in hot oil, being careful to not overcrowd pan. Fry, turning occasionally, until golden brown, 1½ to 2 minutes. (Adjust heat as needed to maintain 360°.) Remove tomatoes using a slotted spoon, and let drain on prepared rack. Serve with Bacon-Buttermilk Dressing. Garnish with reserved bacon, salt, and pepper, if desired.

SOUTHERN POTATO SALAD

Heavy whipping cream makes this potato salad truly decadent.

⚓

YIELD: 8 TO 10 SERVINGS

3   pounds red potatoes, cut into
     1-inch pieces
½   cup mayonnaise
2   tablespoons heavy whipping
     cream
1   tablespoon whole-grain
     mustard
1   teaspoon salt
½   cup chopped celery
3   tablespoons chopped green
     onion
3   tablespoons dill pickle relish
Garnish: chopped green onion

In a large Dutch oven, bring potatoes and water to cover to a boil over medium-high heat. Reduce heat to medium-low; simmer until fork tender, 8 to 10 minutes. Drain, and let cool.

In a large bowl, whisk together mayonnaise, cream, mustard, and salt. Pour over potatoes, stirring gently to combine. Add celery, green onion, and relish, stirring gently to combine. Garnish with green onion, if desired.

QUICK SOUTHERN GREENS

Don't have time to lovingly tend to your greens simmering on the stove for hours?
This version will have your greens ready for the table in a jiffy!

YIELD: 8 TO 10 SERVINGS

1   tablespoon extra-virgin olive oil
1   cup diced yellow onion
1   tablespoon minced fresh garlic
1   smoked ham hock, meat removed from bone and diced
8   cups firmly packed fresh collard greens
8   cups firmly packed fresh turnip greens
2   cups chicken broth
1   tablespoon pepper sauce*
8   cups firmly packed fresh mustard greens
¾   teaspoon kosher salt
⅛   teaspoon ground black pepper

In a large Dutch oven, heat oil over medium-high heat. Add onion, garlic, and ham hock. Cook, stirring occasionally, until onion is softened but not browned, approximately 6 minutes. Add collard and turnip greens, a few handfuls at a time, stirring until wilted after each addition. Add broth and pepper sauce.

Cover and cook for 10 minutes. Stir in mustard greens, salt, and pepper. Cover and cook until greens are just tender, approximately 10 minutes more.

We used Texas Pete.

SPICY CABBAGE SLAW

Chipotle chile powder makes this rainbow of bell peppers and cabbage one to remember.

YIELD: 10 TO 14 SERVINGS

½ head red cabbage, finely shredded

½ head green cabbage, finely shredded

2 red bell peppers, seeded and thinly sliced

2 yellow bell peppers, seeded and thinly sliced

2 green bell peppers, seeded and thinly sliced

⅔ cup fresh orange juice

½ cup olive oil

2 tablespoons white wine vinegar

1 tablespoon sugar

2 teaspoons ground chipotle chile pepper

1 teaspoon salt

½ teaspoon ground black pepper

In a large bowl, combine cabbage and bell peppers. Set aside.

In a small bowl, whisk together orange juice, oil, vinegar, sugar, chile pepper, salt, and pepper. Pour over cabbage mixture, and toss until combined. Cover with plastic wrap, and refrigerate for up to 1 day.

BLT MACARONI SALAD

Turning a lunch-counter favorite into a Southern side has never been easier than this.

---⚓---

YIELD: APPROXIMATELY 16 SERVINGS

¾ cup mayonnaise
¼ cup sour cream
3 tablespoons distilled white vinegar
1 teaspoon kosher salt
1 teaspoon garlic powder
1 teaspoon ground black pepper
1 pound elbow macaroni, cooked according to package directions
8 slices bacon, cooked and crumbled
1 cup grape tomatoes, halved
2 cups roughly chopped romaine lettuce

In a large bowl, stir together mayonnaise, sour cream, vinegar, salt, garlic powder, and pepper until combined. Stir in cooked pasta, bacon, tomatoes, and lettuce. Refrigerate until ready to serve.

BROCCOLI SALAD WITH PECANS

Crunchy and sweet, this salad is bound together with smoky Cheddar cheese and crisp apple.

---⚓---

YIELD: 10 TO 12 SERVINGS

8 cups chopped broccoli (2 large heads)
½ cup diced red onion
½ cup chopped pecans
1 Red Delicious apple, cored and diced
1½ cups shredded smoked Cheddar cheese
¾ cup mayonnaise
2 tablespoons sugar
1½ tablespoons Dijon mustard
1½ tablespoons apple cider vinegar
1 teaspoon kosher salt
¼ teaspoon ground black pepper

In a large bowl, combine broccoli, red onion, pecans, apple, and cheese.

In a small bowl, whisk together mayonnaise and all remaining ingredients. Pour dressing over broccoli mixture, stirring to combine. Refrigerate until ready to serve.

CREAMED CORN

Butter makes everything better. This certainly holds true for this creamed corn recipe.

YIELD: APPROXIMATELY 5 CUPS

18	medium ears fresh corn
3	tablespoons unsalted butter
¾	cup chopped yellow onion
1½	teaspoons kosher salt, divided
¼	cup heavy whipping cream
1	tablespoon chopped fresh thyme
¼	teaspoon ground black pepper
⅛	teaspoon ground red pepper

Holding a long, sharp knife at a downward angle, cut tips from corn kernels (approximately 4 cups). Stand each cob over a large bowl. Using the back of a spoon, scrape downward to remove pulp (approximately 3 cups).

In a 10-inch skillet, melt butter over medium heat. Add onion; cover and cook over medium-low heat until softened, approximately 15 minutes.

Add corn kernel tips, pulp, and 1 teaspoon salt; bring to a boil over medium-high heat. Cover, reduce heat, and simmer, stirring occasionally, until corn is tender, approximately 35 minutes.

Uncover; stir in cream, thyme, black pepper, red pepper, and remaining ½ teaspoon salt. Cook until thickened, 8 to 10 minutes. Serve with extra butter.

CLASSIC SQUASH CASSEROLE

Melty cheese and crispy, buttery crackers top off this casserole full of slightly sweet squash.

---✦---

YIELD: APPROXIMATELY 10 SERVINGS

10 cups sliced yellow squash (approximately 3 pounds)
1½ cups chopped yellow onion
3 cups water
3 cups chicken broth
1 cup shredded Cheddar cheese, divided
½ cup sour cream
½ cup mayonnaise
2 tablespoons unsalted butter, melted and divided
1 teaspoon kosher salt
½ teaspoon ground black pepper
¼ teaspoon garlic powder
1 large egg, lightly beaten
1½ cups crushed buttery round crackers, divided

Preheat oven to 350°. Spray a 2- to 2½-quart baking dish with cooking spray.

In a large Dutch oven, bring squash, onion, 3 cups water, and broth to a boil. Reduce heat to medium-low; simmer until squash is crisp-tender, approximately 7 minutes. Drain well.

In a large bowl, gently stir together squash mixture, ½ cup cheese, sour cream, mayonnaise, 1 tablespoon melted butter, salt, pepper, garlic powder, and egg. Spoon half of squash mixture into prepared pan. Sprinkle with ¾ cup crushed crackers. Top with remaining squash mixture, remaining ¾ cup crushed crackers, and remaining ½ cup cheese. Drizzle with remaining 1 tablespoon melted butter.

Bake until cheese is melted, approximately 25 minutes.

BUTTERBEAN AND CORN SALAD

To save time, this salad can be made up to 2 days ahead.

———————————— ⚜ ————————————

YIELD: APPROXIMATELY 6 SERVINGS

1	pound shelled fresh butterbeans	1	(4-ounce) jar diced pimientos, drained
2½	cups fresh corn kernels (from approximately 5 large ears corn)	¼	cup fresh lemon juice
		3	tablespoons canola oil
⅓	cup chopped red onion	¾	teaspoon salt
2	tablespoons chopped fresh thyme	¼	teaspoon ground black pepper
		Garnish: bacon slices, fresh thyme	

Fill a large saucepan halfway full with water. Bring to a boil over medium-high heat. Add butterbeans; cook for 1 minute. Place in a colander. Rinse under cold running water; drain well.

In a medium bowl, combine butterbeans, corn, onion, thyme, and pimientos. In a small bowl, whisk together lemon juice, oil, salt, and pepper. Pour over corn mixture, stirring to combine. Let stand for at least 10 minutes, or cover and refrigerate for up to 2 days. Garnish with bacon and thyme, if desired.

GRILLED SMASHED NEW POTATOES

Here's a welcome twist on red potatoes: Try them grilled and smashed for a beautiful platter display.

YIELD: APPROXIMATELY 6 SERVINGS

24 small red new potatoes (approximately 1½ pounds)
3 tablespoons olive oil, divided
⅓ cup chopped fresh parsley
1 tablespoon minced fresh garlic
1 teaspoon lemon zest
½ teaspoon kosher salt
¼ teaspoon ground black pepper
1 tablespoon fresh lemon juice

In a large saucepan, bring potatoes and water to cover by 2 inches to a boil over medium-high heat. Cook until the tip of a knife can be easily inserted through potato, 8 to 10 minutes. Drain, and let cool slightly. Using a spatula, gently press until potatoes are just smashed but hold their shape.

Spray grill rack with nonflammable cooking spray. Preheat grill to medium-high heat (350° to 400°).

Brush smashed potatoes with 1 tablespoon oil. Grill, uncovered, until grill marks form on bottom, approximately 2 minutes. Gently turn potatoes; grill 2 minutes more. Transfer to a serving platter. Sprinkle with parsley, garlic, zest, salt, and pepper. Drizzle with lemon juice and remaining 2 tablespoons oil.

SKILLET CORNBREAD

This cornbread is the perfect tool to help get the last bits of delicious Southern fare from your plate to your mouth.

YIELD: APPROXIMATELY 8 SERVINGS

2   cups plain yellow cornmeal
1   cup all-purpose flour
2   teaspoons kosher salt
½   teaspoon baking soda
½   teaspoon baking powder
2   cups whole buttermilk
¼   cup unsalted butter, melted
1   tablespoon honey
2   large eggs, lightly beaten
½   cup fresh corn kernels
2   tablespoons unsalted butter, softened

Preheat oven to 400°. Place a 9-inch cast-iron skillet in oven to preheat.

In a large bowl, whisk together cornmeal, flour, salt, baking soda, and baking powder. In another large bowl, whisk together buttermilk, melted butter, honey, and eggs. Stir buttermilk mixture into cornmeal mixture until combined. Fold in corn.

Carefully remove skillet from oven; add softened butter to pan; let melt. Spoon cornmeal mixture into skillet.

Bake until golden brown, 25 to 30 minutes.

MIDSUMMER SUCCOTASH

Using summer's best produce makes this succotash simply succulent.

---------------------⚜---------------------

YIELD: 10 TO 12 SERVINGS

3	cups fresh baby lima beans
2	cups fresh lady peas
¼	cup butter
2	tablespoons olive oil
¾	cup chopped green onion
1	tablespoon minced garlic
4	cups fresh yellow corn kernels (from approximately 6 ears corn)
2	cups heavy whipping cream
2	tablespoons chopped fresh thyme
1½	teaspoons salt
1	teaspoon sugar
1	teaspoon garlic powder
½	teaspoon ground black pepper
1	pint grape tomatoes, quartered

In a medium saucepan, bring lima beans, lady peas, and water to cover to a boil over medium-high heat. Reduce heat, and cook until tender, 10 to 15 minutes. Drain.

In a Dutch oven or large skillet, heat butter and oil over medium heat until butter is melted. Add green onion and garlic; cook, stirring frequently, for 3 to 4 minutes. Add corn, cooked beans and peas, cream, thyme, salt, sugar, garlic powder, and pepper; cook, stirring occasionally, for 20 minutes.

Add tomatoes, and cook just until heated through, 1 to 2 minutes. Serve immediately.

ROOT BEER BAKED BEANS

This trio of beans gets a hint of sweetness from 2 bottles of root beer,
but is still big on that classic Southern baked bean flavor.

———— ⚓ ————

YIELD: APPROXIMATELY 10 SERVINGS

1	tablespoon vegetable oil
1	cup diced yellow onion
2	cloves garlic, minced
2	(15-ounce) cans pinto beans, rinsed and drained
2	(15-ounce) cans red beans, rinsed and drained
2	(15-ounce) cans cannellini beans, rinsed and drained
2	(12-ounce) bottles root beer
½	cup apple cider vinegar
½	cup ketchup
3	tablespoons firmly packed light brown sugar
2	tablespoons Dijon mustard
2	teaspoons chili powder
1½	teaspoons kosher salt
1	teaspoon ground black pepper

Preheat oven to 400°.

In a large Dutch oven, heat oil over medium-high heat. Add onion; cook, stirring frequently, until just browned, approximately 8 minutes. Add garlic; cook for 1 minute. Stir in beans and all remaining ingredients. Bring to a boil.

Transfer pot to oven, and bake, uncovered, until liquid thickens, approximately 45 minutes. Stir before serving.

SPICY FRIED OKRA

A generous helping of Cajun seasoning and hot sauce gives this okra a lively Acadian flavor.

YIELD: APPROXIMATELY 6 SERVINGS

2   **cups all-purpose flour, divided**
1   **cup plain yellow cornmeal**
1   **tablespoon Cajun seasoning**
1   **cup whole buttermilk**
1   **tablespoon hot sauce**
1   **pound okra, trimmed and halved lengthwise**
Canola oil, for frying
Cajun seasoning, to taste

In a medium bowl, place 1 cup flour. In a large shallow pan, stir together cornmeal, Cajun seasoning, and remaining 1 cup flour. In another large shallow pan, stir together buttermilk and hot sauce.

In a large deep skillet, pour oil to halfway full, and heat over medium-high heat until a deep-fry thermometer registers 350°.

Dredge okra in flour, shaking off excess; dip in buttermilk mixture, letting excess drip off. Dredge in cornmeal mixture, shaking off excess.

Working in batches, carefully add okra to hot oil. Fry, turning occasionally, until golden brown, approximately 3 minutes. (Adjust heat as needed to maintain 350°.) Remove okra from skillet, and let drain on paper towels. Sprinkle with Cajun seasoning, to taste.

CRACKLIN' CORNBREAD

Pork cracklin's gets made over from road trip snack to delicious cornbread
that's a great complement to barbecued meats and other cookout fare.

---A---

YIELD: APPROXIMATELY 8 SERVINGS

1	**(3.5-ounce) bag pork cracklin' strips**
5	**tablespoons bacon drippings, melted and divided**
1	**cup fresh corn kernels (from approximately 1 ear corn)**
½	**cup chopped red bell pepper**
1	**fresh jalapeño, chopped**
1	**cup plain yellow cornmeal**
1	**cup all-purpose flour**
2	**teaspoons baking powder**
1	**teaspoon salt**
¼	**teaspoon baking soda**
1⅓	**cups whole buttermilk**
2	**large eggs**

Preheat oven to 425°.

In a food processor, pulse cracklins until chopped.

In a 10-inch cast-iron skillet, heat 1 tablespoon bacon drippings over medium-high heat. Add corn, bell pepper, and jalapeño; cook for 2 minutes.

In a medium bowl, combine cornmeal, flour, baking powder, salt, and baking soda. Add buttermilk, eggs, and 2 tablespoons bacon drippings. Stir in cracklins and corn mixture.

Add remaining 2 tablespoons bacon drippings to pan. Place in oven until hot, approximately 4 minutes. Carefully spoon batter into hot pan.

Bake until a wooden pick inserted in center comes out clean, approximately 18 minutes. Let cool for 10 minutes before serving.

WATERMELON RIND PICKLES

Once you taste these deliciously sweet and sour pickles, you'll never waste a watermelon rind again.

YIELD: 2 (1-PINT) JARS

1 cup sugar
1 cup water
1 cup Champagne vinegar
1 lemon, sliced
2 teaspoons yellow mustard seeds
1½ teaspoons crushed red pepper
1½ teaspoons kosher salt
1 teaspoon black peppercorns
2 whole star anise
1 stick cinnamon
4 cups cubed peeled watermelon rind

In a medium saucepan, bring sugar, 1 cup water, vinegar, lemon, mustard seeds, red pepper, salt, peppercorns, star anise, and cinnamon to a boil over medium-high heat. Reduce heat to medium-low. Add watermelon rind; simmer until tender, approximately 10 minutes. Remove from heat; let cool in pan for 5 minutes. Discard lemon and cinnamon.

Divide watermelon rind between jars; add vinegar mixture to cover. Seal jars, and let cool to room temperature. Refrigerate for at least 3 hours or up to 1 month.

CORN AND OKRA CORNBREAD STICKS

This playful take on traditional cornbread is made even better with a heavy dose of okra and a hint of Cajun spice.

⚜

YIELD: APPROXIMATELY 18

¼ cup butter
1 cup thinly sliced okra
½ cup fresh corn kernels
1½ tablespoons chopped shallot
1½ teaspoons chopped garlic
1 (6-ounce) package cornbread mix
1 (14.5-ounce) can cream-style corn
½ cup whole buttermilk
3 tablespoons corn oil
1 large egg, lightly beaten
¼ teaspoon Cajun seasoning

Preheat oven to 375°. Spray 3 (6-well) cornbread stick pans with cooking spray, and place in oven to preheat.

In a medium saucepan, melt butter over medium heat. Add okra, corn, shallot, and garlic; cook, stirring frequently, until tender, approximately 8 minutes. Remove from heat.

In a medium bowl, combine cornbread mix, cream-style corn, buttermilk, oil, and egg. Stir in cooked okra mixture. Remove pans from oven, and fill each well approximately three-fourths full with batter.

Bake until golden brown, approximately 30 minutes. Let cool in pans for 10 minutes. Remove corn sticks from pans, and serve warm, or let cool completely on a wire rack.

CHAPTER FIVE

Desserts

SOMETHING SWEET

CLASSIC SOUTHERN POUND CAKE

Sometimes, our taste buds crave simple flavors — that's where this Southern classic fits the bill.

———————— ☙ ————————

YIELD: 10 TO 12 SERVINGS

1	cup unsalted butter, softened
3	cups sugar
6	large eggs
3	cups all-purpose flour
½	teaspoon salt
1½	cups heavy whipping cream
2	teaspoons vanilla extract

Spray a 15-cup Bundt pan with baking spray with flour.

In a large bowl, beat butter and sugar with a mixer at medium speed until fluffy, 3 to 4 minutes, stopping to scrape sides of bowl. Add eggs, one at a time, beating well after each addition.

In a medium bowl, sift together flour and salt. With mixer on low speed, gradually add flour mixture to butter mixture alternately with cream, beginning and ending with flour mixture, beating just until combined after each addition. Beat in vanilla.

Spoon batter into prepared pan; tap pan on counter twice to release any air bubbles. Place in a cold oven.

Bake at 325° until a wooden pick inserted near center comes out clean, about 1 hour and 10 minutes. Let cool in pan for 10 minutes. Remove from pan, and let cool completely on a wire rack.

PEANUT BUTTER PIE

Classic peanut butter flavor blends beautifully with this pie's cinnamon graham cracker crust. Its simplicity is hard to resist.

YIELD: 1 (9-INCH) PIE

1   (5-ounce) sleeve cinnamon graham crackers (about 9 whole crackers)
1   cup roasted salted peanuts
2   tablespoons granulated sugar
6   tablespoons butter, slightly softened
1½   cups creamy peanut butter
1   (8-ounce) package cream cheese, softened
1   cup confectioners' sugar, sifted
2   cups heavy whipping cream
Garnish: chopped peanuts, sweetened whipped cream

Preheat oven to 350°. Spray a 9-inch pie plate with cooking spray.

In the work bowl of a food processor, pulse together graham crackers, peanuts, and granulated sugar until finely ground, 5 or 6 times. Add butter; pulse until combined, 3 or 4 times. Reserve 1 tablespoon crumb mixture for garnish. Using a measuring cup, press remaining mixture into bottom and up sides of prepared plate.

Bake until lightly browned, about 10 minutes. Let cool completely.

In a large bowl, beat peanut butter and cream cheese with a mixer at medium speed until smooth. Add confectioners' sugar, beating to combine. Reduce mixer speed to low; beat in cream. Increase mixer speed to high; beat just until thickened. Spread filling into prepared crust.

Cover and refrigerate until firm, about 4 hours. Garnish with reserved 1 tablespoon crust mixture, peanuts, and whipped cream, if desired.

BLUEBERRY CRUMB BARS

Sweet, fresh blueberries sandwiched between a crumbly butter crust makes these portable bars a no-brainer.

---☆---

YIELD: APPROXIMATELY 12

3   cups all-purpose flour
2   cups old-fashioned oats
2   cups granulated sugar, divided
½   cup firmly packed light brown sugar
1   tablespoon lemon zest
1   teaspoon baking powder
¼   teaspoon salt
1   cup cold unsalted butter, cubed
1   large egg
2   tablespoons fresh lemon juice
4   teaspoons cornstarch
4   cups fresh blueberries

Preheat oven to 375°. Spray a 13x9-inch baking pan with baking spray with flour.

In a medium bowl, combine flour, oats, 1 cup granulated sugar, brown sugar, zest, baking powder, and salt. Using a pastry blender, cut in butter and egg until mixture is crumbly. Press half of dough into prepared pan.

In another medium bowl, stir together lemon juice, cornstarch, and remaining 1 cup granulated sugar. Gently fold in blueberries. Spread blueberry mixture over dough. Crumble remaining dough over berries.

Bake until lightly browned, 35 to 45 minutes. Let cool completely before cutting into bars.

CARAMEL-PECAN SHEET CAKE

Feeding a crowd? Caramel frosting and pecans take this basic sheet cake to a whole new level.

YIELD: 10 TO 12 SERVINGS

SHEET CAKE

1 cup butter
1 cup water
2 cups all-purpose flour
2 cups sugar
1 teaspoon baking soda
½ teaspoon salt
¼ teaspoon ground cinnamon
¼ teaspoon ground ginger
½ cup sour cream
2 large eggs
1 teaspoon vanilla extract
Caramel Frosting (recipe follows)
1 cup toasted pecans, chopped

CARAMEL FROSTING

½ cup butter
1 cup firmly packed light brown sugar
½ teaspoon salt
½ cup sour cream
2½ cups confectioners' sugar
½ teaspoon vanilla extract

FOR CAKE: Preheat oven to 325°. Spray a 15x10-inch jelly-roll pan with baking spray with flour.

In a medium saucepan, bring butter and 1 cup water to a boil. Remove from heat.

In a large bowl, whisk together flour, sugar, baking soda, salt, cinnamon, and ginger. Add hot butter mixture to flour mixture; beat with a mixer at low speed just until moistened. Beat in sour cream. Add eggs, one at a time, beating well after each addition. Stir in vanilla. Pour batter into prepared pan.

Bake until lightly browned and a wooden pick inserted in center comes out clean, 25 to 30 minutes. Let cool for 20 minutes.

FOR CARAMEL FROSTING: In a large saucepan, bring butter, brown sugar, and salt to a boil over medium heat, stirring constantly. Remove from heat; gradually stir in sour cream. Bring just to a boil, stirring constantly. Remove from heat.

Gradually add confectioners' sugar and vanilla, beating with a mixer at medium speed until smooth. Use immediately.

Pour hot Caramel Frosting over warm cake. Sprinkle with pecans. Let cool completely on a wire rack.

STRAWBERRY ICEBOX PIE

Creamy and cool, this strawberry pie is the perfect treat to combat the dreaded Southern heat.

YIELD: 1 (9-INCH) PIE

1	(11-ounce) box vanilla wafers	4	tablespoons confectioners' sugar, divided
½	cup unsalted butter, melted	1	teaspoon vanilla extract
1	cup fresh strawberries, hulled	½	cup crème fraîche
½	lemon, juiced	½	cup mascarpone
3	tablespoons granulated sugar	3	large pasteurized egg whites, chilled
1½	cups heavy whipping cream		Garnish: fresh mint

Spray a 10-inch springform pan with cooking spray.

In the work bowl of a food processor, place vanilla wafers and melted butter; pulse until mixture is crumbly. Firmly press into bottom and slightly up sides of prepared pan. Refrigerate for 20 minutes.

In the container of a blender, place strawberries, lemon juice, and granulated sugar. Process until smooth; set aside.

In a medium bowl, beat cream, 2 tablespoons confectioners' sugar, and vanilla with a mixer at high speed until stiff peaks form.

In another medium bowl, beat crème fraîche and mascarpone with a mixer at high speed until combined. Add crème fraîche mixture to whipped cream mixture, and beat at medium speed until combined.

In a third medium bowl, using clean beaters, beat egg whites at high speed until soft peaks form. Add remaining 2 tablespoons confectioners' sugar, and beat until stiff peaks form. Gently fold egg whites into whipped cream mixture. Fold in half of strawberry purée; spread over prepared crust. Spoon remainder of strawberry purée over top, and swirl using a wooden pick. Cover with foil, and freeze for at least 2 hours or up to 5 days. Remove from freezer 15 minutes before serving. Garnish with mint, if desired.

CREAMY CHOCOLATE ICEBOX PIE

This dreamy icebox treat is beyond simple to whip up on a whim or for a cookout filled with guests.

YIELD: 1 (9-INCH) PIE

CHOCOLATE CRUST
2   cups crushed chocolate
      sandwich cookies*
¼   cup unsalted butter, melted

FILLING
¼   cup heavy whipping cream
½   cup semisweet chocolate
      morsels
1   (3.9-ounce) box chocolate
      instant pudding mix
1⅓ cups whole buttermilk

Garnish: whipped topping,
          unsweetened cocoa powder

FOR CRUST: Preheat oven to 350°.

In a medium bowl, stir together crushed cookies and melted butter. Using a measuring cup, press mixture into bottom and up sides of a 9-inch pie plate.

Bake until set, about 8 minutes. Let cool completely on a wire rack.

FOR FILLING: In a small bowl, microwave cream until very hot, about 1 minute. Add chocolate morsels, stirring until smooth. Pour chocolate mixture into prepared crust. Refrigerate until firm, about 15 minutes.

In a large bowl, whisk together pudding mix and buttermilk until smooth. Spoon pudding into crust, smoothing top with an offset spatula. Place a piece of plastic wrap directly on surface of filling. Refrigerate until firm, about 3 hours. Garnish with whipped topping and cocoa, if desired.

We used Oreos.

CORNMEAL-BUTTERMILK SHORTCAKES WITH GRILLED PEACHES

A down-home twist on the classic pairing with strawberries, this version is packed with summery flavor.

⚓

YIELD: 8 SERVINGS

1½ cups all-purpose flour
½ cup plain yellow cornmeal
2 tablespoons plus 1½ teaspoons sugar, divided
1½ teaspoons baking powder
½ teaspoon salt
6 tablespoons cold unsalted butter, cubed
¾ cup plus 2 tablespoons whole buttermilk, divided
1 large egg, lightly beaten
8 ripe peaches, peeled, pitted, and halved
1 tablespoon canola oil
½ cup butter, melted
1 cup peach preserves
Sweetened whipped cream, to serve

Preheat oven to 425°. Line a baking sheet with parchment paper.

In the work bowl of a food processor, pulse flour, cornmeal, 2 tablespoons sugar, baking powder, and salt 3 times. Add cold butter; pulse until butter is the size of small peas, 4 or 5 times. Spoon mixture into a bowl; stir in ¾ cup buttermilk and egg until moistened. (Add remaining 2 tablespoons buttermilk, if needed).

Spoon dough onto prepared pan. Using floured hands, press into an 8-inch circle. Using a serrated knife dipped in flour, score dough into 8 wedges, cutting into dough ¼ inch. (Do not cut completely through dough.) Sprinkle with remaining 1½ teaspoons sugar.

Bake until golden brown, 16 to 18 minutes. Let cool completely on a wire rack.

Lightly spray a grill rack with nonflammable cooking spray. Preheat grill to medium heat (300° to 350°).

Brush peach halves with oil. Grill, cut side down, until peaches can be easily turned, about 2 minutes. Turn peaches; cook 2 minutes more.

Using a serrated knife, cut shortcake into 8 wedges. Cut each wedge in half horizontally. Spread cut sides with melted butter and preserves. Brush peaches with preserves. Place peach halves on bottoms of shortcakes. Top with shortcake tops. Serve with whipped cream.

VANILLA BEAN BANANA PUDDING

In this pudding, vanilla bean gets to join in on the fun with the bananas and vanilla wafers. This is a Southern classic, pure and simple.

YIELD: APPROXIMATELY 12 SERVINGS

8	large eggs, separated
2	cups sugar, divided
½	cup all-purpose flour
⅛	teaspoon salt
4½	cups whole milk
1	vanilla bean, split lengthwise, seeds scraped and reserved
1	tablespoon butter
1	(11-ounce) package vanilla wafers
6	ripe bananas, sliced
½	teaspoon cream of tartar

Preheat oven to 375°.

In a large bowl, whisk together egg yolks and 1 cup sugar.

In a large saucepan, combine flour and salt; whisk in milk and vanilla bean seeds. Bring to a simmer over medium heat, stirring constantly. Remove from heat. Stir half of hot milk mixture into egg yolk mixture. Stir egg yolk mixture into remaining hot milk mixture in pan. Cook over medium heat, stirring constantly, until mixture comes to a simmer. Cook, stirring constantly, until thickened, about 2 minutes. Remove from heat. Stir in butter until melted.

In a shallow 3-quart baking dish, layer half of vanilla wafers, half of banana slices, and half of vanilla pudding. Repeat layers once.

In a large bowl, beat egg whites and cream of tartar with a mixer at high speed until foamy. Gradually add remaining 1 cup sugar, beating just until stiff peaks form. Spoon over pudding, spreading to seal edges.

Bake until lightly browned, 10 to 12 minutes. Let cool for 30 minutes on a wire rack. Serve warm, or refrigerate for up to 4 hours.

EASY LEMON ICEBOX PIE

Cream cheese and sweetened condensed milk cuts the lemony zest of this icebox pie with refreshing ease.

YIELD: 1 (9-INCH) PIE

4   ounces cream cheese, softened
1   (14-ounce) can sweetened
    condensed milk
1   tablespoon lemon zest
½   cup fresh lemon juice
1   cup frozen whipped topping,
    thawed
1   (6-ounce) package graham
    cracker piecrust
Garnish: whipped topping, lemon
    slices, fresh mint

In a large bowl, beat cream cheese with a mixer at medium speed until smooth. Add condensed milk and lemon zest and juice, beating until combined. Fold in whipped topping. Spoon filling into prepared crust, smoothing top with an offset spatula.

Cover and refrigerate until firm, about 3 hours or up to 3 days. Garnish with whipped topping, lemon slices, and mint, if desired.

WATERMELON-CANTALOUPE ICE POPS

Ice pops aren't just for kids! This colorful treat is sure to make a fun statement at your next get-together.

YIELD: APPROXIMATELY 10

3 cups diced seedless watermelon

1¼ cups sugar, divided

4 tablespoons fresh lemon juice, divided

2 tablespoons light corn syrup, divided

3 cups seeded and diced cantaloupe

In the container of a blender, combine watermelon, ½ cup plus 2 tablespoons sugar, 2 tablespoons lemon juice, and 1 tablespoon corn syrup. Blend on high speed until completely smooth. Strain mixture through a fine-mesh sieve into a medium bowl, pressing solids to extract as much liquid as possible. Discard solids, and set watermelon liquid aside. Repeat blending and straining procedure with cantaloupe, remaining ½ cup plus 2 tablespoons sugar, remaining 2 tablespoons lemon juice, and remaining 1 tablespoon corn syrup.

Fill 10 (3-ounce) plastic ice pop molds halfway with cantaloupe mixture. Freeze until firm, about 1 hour. Fill molds with watermelon mixture, and freeze until solid, about 4 hours.

PEACH COBBLER

Does anything say "summer" quite as well as a bubbling pan of peach cobbler?

---⚓---

YIELD: APPROXIMATELY 6 SERVINGS

CLASSIC CRUST

1   cup all-purpose flour
2   teaspoons sugar
¼   teaspoon salt
¼   cup cold butter, cubed
1   tablespoon all-vegetable shortening
3 to 4 tablespoons ice water

COBBLER

5   cups (¾ inch thick) sliced fresh peaches (approximately 6 medium peaches)
⅓   cup firmly packed light brown sugar
2   tablespoons all-purpose flour
½   teaspoon ground cinnamon
⅛   teaspoon ground nutmeg
⅛   teaspoon salt
2   tablespoons unsalted butter, cubed
2   teaspoons fresh lemon juice
1   tablespoon heavy whipping cream
2   teaspoons granulated sugar

FOR CRUST: In the work bowl of a food processor, combine flour, sugar, and salt; pulse 3 times. Add butter and shortening; pulse until mixture is crumbly, 4 to 6 times. Spoon mixture into a bowl; add ice water, 1 tablespoon at a time, tossing just until moistened. Shape dough into a disk, and wrap in plastic wrap. Refrigerate for 30 minutes.

On a lightly floured surface, roll dough into an 11-inch circle. Cut dough into 8 strips.

FOR COBBLER: Preheat oven to 375°.

In a 10-inch cast-iron or stainless steel skillet, toss together peaches, brown sugar, flour, cinnamon, nutmeg, and salt. Sprinkle with butter and lemon juice.

Arrange 4 strips of Classic Crust, spacing evenly apart, over filling. Arrange remaining 4 strips crosswise over first dough strips. Trim excess dough; gently press edges of dough to skillet. Brush dough with cream, and sprinkle with granulated sugar.

Bake until filling is bubbly and crust is lightly browned, about 35 minutes. Let cool on a wire rack for 20 minutes before serving.

COCONUT CREAM PIE

Tropical coconut notes will whisk you away for a mental holiday on a white,
sandy beach with this pie. Go ahead and indulge!

---✿---

YIELD: 1 (9-INCH) PIE

BUTTERMILK CRUST
- 1¼ cups all-purpose flour
- 1 teaspoon kosher salt
- 1 teaspoon sugar
- ½ cup cold unsalted butter, cubed
- 4 tablespoons whole buttermilk, chilled

PIE
- ½ cup plus 6 tablespoons sugar, divided
- 3 tablespoons cornstarch
- ⅛ teaspoon kosher salt
- 1 cup whole milk
- 1½ cups unsweetened coconut milk, divided
- 4 large egg yolks
- 1 cup sweetened flaked coconut
- 1 teaspoon vanilla extract
- 1½ cups heavy whipping cream
- Garnish: toasted sweetened flaked coconut

FOR CRUST: Preheat oven to 350°.

In a medium bowl, stir together flour, salt, and sugar. Using a pastry blender or 2 forks, cut in butter until mixture is crumbly. Add buttermilk, 1 tablespoon at a time, stirring until a dough forms. Turn out dough onto a lightly floured surface, and shape into a disk. Wrap tightly in plastic wrap, and refrigerate until firm, at least 30 minutes.

On a lightly floured surface, roll dough into a 12-inch circle. Transfer to a 9-inch pie plate, pressing into bottom and up sides. Fold edges under, and crimp as desired. Top with a piece of parchment paper, letting ends extend over edges of plate. Add pie weights.

Bake for 20 minutes. Carefully remove paper and weights. Bake until golden brown, about 8 minutes more. Let cool for 20 minutes on a wire rack.

FOR PIE: In a medium saucepan, combine ½ cup sugar, cornstarch, and salt; whisk in milk, 1 cup coconut milk, and egg yolks. Cook over medium heat, stirring constantly, until thickened, about 10 minutes. Remove from heat. Stir in coconut and vanilla.

Spoon filling into prepared crust. Let cool for 10 minutes. Place a piece of plastic wrap directly on surface of filling. Refrigerate until firm, about 3 hours.

In a large bowl, beat cream and remaining 6 tablespoons sugar with a mixer at high speed until soft peaks form. Add remaining ½ cup coconut milk. Beat until stiff peaks form, about 1 minute.

Top with coconut whipped cream, and garnish with coconut, if desired.

RECIPE INDEX

SEAFOOD

SWEETS